I0755568

Old Too Fast, Smart Too Late

OLD TOO FAST, SMART TOO LATE

A Prisoner's Foolish Journey to Wisdom

Arlando "Tray" Jones III

First Edition

Casebound ISBN: 978-1-62720-238-1
Paperback ISBN: 978-1-62720-239-8
Ebook ISBN: 978-1-62720-240-4

Printed in the United States of America

Design by Molly Werts
Development by Keelin Ferdinandsen
Edited by Marc Morjé Howard
Promotion by Erin Russell

Published by Apprentice House Press

Apprentice House Press
Loyola University Maryland
4501 N. Charles Street
Baltimore, MD 21210
410.617.5265 • 410.617.2198 (fax)
www.ApprenticeHouse.com
info@ApprenticeHouse.com

Preface

It must be known that my sole allegiance is to the truth. Hence, everything I say I am — I am. How many among us can say, "if you don't lie on me, I won't tell the truth about you?" It's a mighty joy to live an authentic life.

If I sound angry or arrogant, fuck it! That's what I am — angry and arrogant. Thirty-four (34) years ago it was cruelly demonstrated to me what it means to be superfluous. Before that, I thought I was the shit. When I was uptown, in costly and-free society, when a nigga would ask me, "What's happening?" My answer would often be, "You know me, I eat steak, sleep late, read comic books, count money, and laugh real funny."

One night, I'm outside hangin', doing my dope dealin' thing. I see Cam — and I asked him about some money that was in dispute. He gave me a wrong answer. So I punched him in the mouth.

Cam silly ass didn't acquiesce. The motherfucka dared to hit me back while Mississippi was standing right there with me. 'Sip put seven hot ones in that nigga. Case closed. That is what happened. I've been in prison 34 years for that.

The hardest part of my journey is to watch my cousin, my co-defendant — Eric Hunter — spend this ungodly amount of time in prison with me, for a crime he absolutely didn't commit. Eric wasn't even there…

How can I not, sometimes, be angry? I was rendered superfluous in a world that demands that you be somebody.

I learned the word "superfluous" as a global concept from my friend, Professor Marc Howard. He brought me an opportunity to break from prison's restrictive prism.

Marc acquainted me with Hannah Arendt. She taught that totalitarian rule demands that members or segments of a society must be made to feel superfluous. In India, it was and remains the "Untouchables." In America, it's the nigga. It's me! Hitler's Germany, Stalin's Russia, the list is endless of what my grandfather, father and I have always faced: the oppressive and stifling weight of totalitarian authority.

America isn't as overt in her execution of totalitarian rule. But I'm familiar with Nietzsche's observation: "A man who fails to recognize the hand that kills with leniency has lived life foolishly." (I, without doubt, mauled the exact quote. Alas, Nietzsche spoke German—and I speak to the shibboleth.)

Anyway, my book starts off as "dark." I know, when I first started this project, Marc told me, "Tray, you need to quit that fuckin' job."

I had sometimes shown up to class emotionally and spiritually drained from my stints/shifts on hospice care work. Whenever my shine is threatened, I take heed. Need I say, I quit my sole money paying job just 'cause Marc observed that the work was diminishing me.

That's not all true, of course. But we should note that, "If the lion doesn't tell his story, the hunter will get all the credit."

I want to explain why my book starts off seemingly "dark." I was, perhaps, going through a dark time. I was reconciling myself with my own eschatology. What would my epitaph say? I am determined to write my own ending.

If I were in an exclusively angry place when I started this project, you would find me tedious and unworthy of your time and attention. For only one letter separates anger and danger. Thus, one would be wise to distance himself/herself from an angry man. He is a danger.

Alas, the world is plagued with evils. Marc's course underscored (for me, at least) man's constant and consistent quest to conquer. America is so flippant and vainglorious, it uses loans through the International Monetary Fund (IMF) to bribe small, desperate nations. Professor Jimmy Ray Vreeland said a Russian associate of his told him that bribes are common in his country. Corruption is rampant in Russia. Tough guys are all over Russia. But ain't nobody as gangster tough as America. She uses loans—money that must be paid back—to execute bribes. "That's gangsta." That's how a totalitarian rules.

It's my fiercely held belief that poverty is the most violent act that can be inflicted upon a people or person. Poverty makes for desperation and shame.

America stands unique in her "unusually cruel" practice of mass incarceration. No one is better at explaining and describing America's most obscene practice, without using a single obscenity, than Marc. (I pray that he introduces some light to my dark experience.)

Oh well, I write this book because I want it to be known that love is, in fact, the greatest and grandest tool for man. I can attest to the fact that victory in life is realized when you experience life's worst and cruelest, yet emerge loving and lovable.

Describe your experience; define your own life. Know that what you can't describe, recognize, and/or define will have a greater impact and influence over you than you'll have over it. For instance, knowing that a vital element of totalitarian rule is to be able to render segments of its population superfluous makes it essential to each individual to develop a craft, or some skill set, a good and/or service that will keep you relevant. If you don't believe a thing I say, please believe it when I say: it's best to die ten years too early than to live ten minutes too long.

If you submit to anger and all the hatefulness, resentment, and bitterness that it can rot, you leave yourself unnecessarily vulnerable to a totalitarian rule that's maintained by making some folks superfluous

What more can I say? To have been under the influence and tutelage of professors Marc Howard, Drew Leder, and Fr. Tim Brown for several years is to have your mind stretched. And we know what Aristotle said about a mind stretched: "It can never return to its original dimension."

There was a time when I felt an abiding shame for allowing myself to come to prison. "I'd rather be dead in my grave then to be a slave," my paternal step grandfather would sing. He was born in 1892 — and fought in World War I, The Great War. Daddy, my grandfather, had no love for America. He didn't fight for America from a sense of patriotism; he fought because a black man — then and now — has to go to extraordinary lengths to avoid convict-leasing (now "mass incarceration") — an enterprise that was arguably worse than slavery.

Anyway, Daddy reared my father to accept the grave before the cage. "Don't let them white people lock you in no cage," was the stern warning. Would that I got the grave rather than the cage, you would not be getting this jewel. My greatest regret: I had to get old too fast and smart too late before I can get this revelation to you.

Chapter I

Death Gives Everything Except Answers

When you face death, the meaning of life becomes clear, defined. If death frightens you or provokes anxiety within you, life will be far more challenging. I don't deny the fact that dying is a terrifying thing. Only the most psychologically disturbed or mentally troubled among us will approach the end with ease.

Death is the greatest mystery of all. No amount of man's sophisticated theorizing or philosophizing has been able to satisfy our concerns and fears about death. When we die, do we go to hell or heaven, with respect to how morally or immorally we lived? What is hell like? Do we burn throughout eternity as our Sunday School teachers taught? If I give the hobos sleeping on the streets the shirt off my back, honor my vows of fidelity to my wife, and live an utterly selfless life, will I go to heaven? Moreover, what is heaven?

No empirical or existential information is available to answer any of these questions. Astronauts have gone into outer space, scientists have examined the entire earth and yet no one has been able to provide us with a universally acceptable answer about death. That said, it is still a given that the universe and all within it hate secrets.

Thus, the universe conspires to reveal all that is hidden. It won't happen as a revelation. The universe rotates or sits still and follows her nature and allows you to figure it out. But death remains elusive and mysterious and demands that you extinguish your life before she discloses herself to you. To do otherwise might prompt us to shy away from our destinies.

Death's secret is seemingly too much for our vanity, for our human pride to bear. Our fancy and sophisticated philosophies and theologies have provided convincing theories for each of life's phenomena, except death. How is it that a benevolent Creator provides us with this one thing in common?

We don't all receive great parents, good health, abundant wealth, an attractive temperament and so on. We are not born or created equal. We come into fruition with different challenges and different abilities with which we meet our challenges. We will all suffer, of course, in accordance with Buddhism's First Noble Truth, because we desire things that we don't possess. The one thing that we do possess is a promised end.

Once we die, will we return, as in reincarnation? Are we already reincarnated beings who don't remember our former lives? There is a plethora of questions and not a single universally acceptable answer.

I am convinced that the same day that we are given a birthday, we are given a day on which we will die. One of these dates is made known to us, but we cannot possibly know the other until it occurs. Hence, it looms over us and haunts us. We give craven pause when and where we should be spontaneous and bold because death's uncertainty fills us with anxiety.

If you are blessed, as I am blessed, you will find a way to reconcile your fears with death. You will reach a point where you will accept that in this life, you can know absolutely nothing about what is going to happen after you die and simply find satisfaction in knowing that a Benevolent Creator, a Merciful and exceedingly Good Being gives to us all a single thing that will capture Its goodness and mercy.

Death's mystery is beyond our sophistication and vanity. It defies definition, but becomes a welcomed friend when our bodies break down and offer us nothing aside from agonizing pain. Sometimes our psyche breaks and we feel an excruciating hopelessness and death appears to us as an out from life's pain and suffering. We conclude that life is hard; life is undeniable suffering. Death is then viewed in a lens of honesty and courage.

Hakim

I requested an assignment of hospice care work at Jessup Correctional Institution because I felt that it would be easy work. I would earn $1.05 per day without having to compete with anyone seeking my job. Moreover, I wouldn't have to maneuver the various personalities of supervisors. It would simply be me and whoever I had to watch die. Prison is a cold and callous place; death is a constant. For many of us, death is better than a life of prison.

When I was told, on July 25, a Saturday night, that I would have to go sit with Hakim, my very good friend, I was somewhat apprehensive. I knew that Hakim was on his last legs. He had been battling a kidney disease for well over a decade. The fact that his body's organs were finally shutting down was no surprise to me. I wanted to see how Hakim would face his death. He had sent others to their death and seemed to look at death from that perspective with a casual calmness, for there is a dichotomy between the killer and the killed. Hakim had once told me, "Death ain't nothing. We all gotta go."

In retrospect, I wanted to see for myself if this man, whom I, without equivocation, considered my friend, would die. Would he boldly and courageously walk into the abyss? Hakim was a soldier.

He had navigated the vicious and uncompromising ghetto streets and treacherous penitentiary tiers in an honorable and dignified way. He died with as much dignity as the horrendous and dirty conditions of the prison's hospice would allow.

I was very familiar with Isolation Ward 2 at the Jessup Regional Hospital. I had been there several times. It is frequently used as the hospice, but prior to actually sitting in there with Hakim, I hadn't taken notice of how abysmally dirty, dark and lonely that small hospital room was. Dust-mites or dust-bunnies littered the upper portion of the walls and corners of the room. The fluorescent lights glowed dimly. There was not a single bright space in Ward 2. It was a sorry excuse for the end.

Ward 2 is perhaps a hidden blessing. It speaks to the dying man in a harsh way, but with a comforting truth. There is nothing more to cling to; let us proceed into the abyss. It is time to discover if the stories offered in our holy texts are true.

Hakim laid helplessly in bed while Tyrone sat in a chair next him reading from the Bible.

"Man, what'n the fuck is wrong with you?" I said to Tyrone in as quiet and subdued a manner as possible.

"You know Hakim is Muslim. If you gotta read some scriptures to him, it should be from the Koran."

I had noticed the annoyance and agitation in Hakim's eyes when I first entered the room. In an instant, I understood Hakim's troubled state. Hakim and I had been friends for more than thirty years. Tyrone's form of passive Christian worship was an abomination to him. If Hakim could've spoken, he would have used every vituperative phrase he could think of to condemn Tyrone for attempting to impose his religious beliefs. But Hakim could only lie there in bed motionless and mute. He was an apparition of his former virile self. Hakim's only means of communication was through the steel and fire in his eyes.

Once I cursed Tyrone and ushered him from Hakim's presence, a sparkle appeared in Hakim's eyes. He was silently laughing.

"Damn, Hakim," My anger toward Tyrone was gone. I felt only an overwhelming and all-consuming love for my friend. "What you need me to do or be?"

Hakim stared at me. He seemed to be amused by my apprehension and affection. My philosophies and theories offered no guidepost for this delicate moment.

This was death's domain. No eloquent words or clever phrases would do. The only scriptures that mattered were the ones inscribed in my heart and shared by our collective soul.

My friend was Muslim, yes, but not a very devout one. I was a Christian and also not devout. We were both 'hood. Our strongest and most impressionable life lessons came from the hardships of poverty, crime, ghetto streets, and the penitentiary. Life had proven to be harsh to both of us. The lessons in the

Bible and Koran may have eluded us, but Buddha's First Noble Truth sure haunted our existence.

I reached out and grabbed Hakim's hand. I held it in mine and told him, "I know you ain't into no sentimental shit. Me neither, nigga. But I love you, man, and I'm gonna miss you when you gone. That is for sure."

Hakim closed his eyes. Tears followed and I wiped them away and told him, "I'm just gonna sit here with you. If you need me to do anything, blink your eyes, fart, or do something to let me know." But I ain't going nowhere 'til I gotta."

We sat there in silence. He became Christ, and I was his loyal disciple. Our Gethsemane had no grass or trees. None of the calming natural beauty of a garden surrounded Hakim and me. We were not innocent men being pursued for persecution for righteousness sake. But we agonized in our own way. The only tool I had, the only comfort I could summon, was love.

My work as a hospice care worker was proving to be far more emotionally and psychologically taxing than I had anticipated. And yet, holding hands and sitting silently with a dying man endowed me with a divine blessing. That blessing is wisdom, but humility won't permit me to make that declaration.

*****

I took it as an omen when Hakim died on July 27, 2015, which was on the forty seventh anniversary of my birth. When news reached me that my friend and very first hospice care patient had passed away on my birthday, I couldn't contain my amusement and joy. I was reassured that I had, indeed, been given a divine gift. I was given, through my time with Hakim the opportunity to come into the profundity of death and glean its greatest lessons.

All I did was sit with Hakim and steadfastly direct my focus and attention to him. I felt absolute compassion for him and held no judgment. My epiphany came. I must love more than I am loved and be okay with that. I intuitively knew from that moment forward that I would have to be a greater friend to the people that came into my life than they would be friends to me. My all will be enough.

It is essential that I do not reduce love to romantic notions; its power is much more significant than physical and emotional attachments. Let love simply be love. Do not reduce it to a definition. And, for God's sake, don't let love become a business arrangement, that is, loving someone only if he or she loves you in return or meets some other expectation.

Rick

My second hospice care patient, Rick, allowed me to have a more profound appreciation for what hospice care work entailed. Rick had been fighting cancer for eight years and he wanted to live. He never wanted to stop breathing, though he knew that at some point he would. However, he was determined to endure all the painful treatment of chemotherapy and radiation necessary to prolong his life.

Rick grew up Catholic and he harbored guilt about damn near everything. He needed time, all that the universe would give to him, to settle things on earth. Rick said that he had committed more wrongs against others than others had committed against him.

“You want me to take that cord and whip you on the back like some of ‘em crazy ass monks do so you can pay up for all your sins?” I had jokingly asked Rick.

He and I were talking about Opus Dei, an order within the Catholic Church rumored to inflict physical torture upon themselves.

“Nah, man, I’m in enough pain,” Rick admitted. “I just wanna find a way to stop hating my younger brother.”

My time with Rick was completely different from that which I spent with Hakim. Rick was a talker. When he wasn’t nauseated from chemotherapy, he used his energy to talk, laugh, and summon as much joy from his last days as he possibly could. He had been sentenced to three consecutive life terms of imprisonment. Rick understood that his crimes were so heinous and hideous that mortal men could never grant him expiation. He was okay with that reality.

“Tray, I wish people could forgive me and not hate me so that they could go on and have better lives,” Rick once said to me. He was being sincere and I was reminded of just how Christ was sincere in his plea to God to “Forgive them Father; they know not what they do.”

The Gospel tells us that when Jesus was nailed to the cross, he prayed for those responsible for his unjust torture. That was not the situation with Rick. He and I were typical convicts, hardened criminals. Rick grew up in a typical middle-class, white Catholic household.

His mother, according to Rick, was a saint. She tolerated a drunk, philandering husband and did her very best to rear four children. Rick’s youngest brother had swindled their mother out of her home and life’s savings. In her elder years, Rick’s mom lived as a pauper in a house filled with squalor. She had been abandoned, and Rick blamed his youngest brother. He wanted to kill him, but his saintly mother wouldn't hear of it.

It was about 2:30 or 3:00 in the morning and I had been on duty as a hospice care worker since nine o'clock that evening. My relief, the hospice care worker designated to take my place at one had fallen ill. Rick was thoroughly pleased about that. He was feeling alright. The agonizing physical pain you'd associate with imminent death wasn't bothering him at that time. It was time to engage the resident philosopher (me)in a conversation that would challenge my intimate beliefs.

"Why can't I forgive my brother?" was the question that gnawed at Rick. He was dying, and hell was a reality to him. The hatred that Rick felt toward his brother was palpable and stood as the central barrier to his entrance into heaven.

I don't see Jesus through the image that's commonly given. The scriptures that were narrated during Sunday sermons seemed like hollow and empty platitudes. In my heart, in a light quiet place within my soul, an image of Jesus becomes real to me. He is not with twelve other men sitting around a boardroom like table enjoying a Lucullan feasts. They're divine, colorless, souls. My Lord and Savior is sitting at the table with his twelve disciples, and Peter, Jesus' most beloved, says to him, "Jesus, you're my man. I love you. I am completely loyal and devoted to you." This image may change in my mind to serve certain life challenges when I am called to appreciate and understand loyalty in a loving way.

Jesus looks at Peter with love and absolute understanding, "Peter, you gonna deny knowing me three times before the rooster crow."

Jesus understood Peter's weaknesses and frailties, but he didn't refer to Peter as a weak-ass-punk. He loved Peter. Jesus' manner of love was revolutionary and not for the faint of heart. Jesus loved Peter because he loved Peter. There was no need for reciprocity. For love, according to Levine and echoing Jesus' teaching is the only rational act. God sent Jesus to man to teach us how to love through love. However, we reduced love to some kind of business deal. Jesus epitomized love.

The Poet, Auden, put it best when he wrote: Love each other or perish. But holding on to past hurts and wrongs prevent us from loving without preconditions.

"Peter, you're going to be the cornerstone for which I build my church."

If my homie was to deny knowing me, I would reciprocate. My ego demands recognition. It holds my hubris expectations.

Judas was at that table too. He was there for Christ's last supper, and I'm more than certain that he pledged his devotion and loyalty to Jesus in equal measure.

"Jesus, you're my man, I'm with you 'til the end. I'd never cross you." Jesus and the Father are One. We can't hide the secrets that are in our hearts from him. The Lord knew that Judas was going to rat him out to the Romans and that he'd be persecuted, crucified, and abandoned, but Jesus still loved him. The people that I dealt with would kill you if they suspected you'd turn them in to be arrested and I would've gladly joined them.

"When you love somebody, Rick, you give him two things: the power to destroy you and the trust not to," I told Rick. I didn't know where it came from or when I had heard it. It was in my heart and I felt compelled to communicate it to him. Love presents us with one of life's most complex riddle. Perhaps it's a paradox that can't be figured out. It has to be lived out.

If you're hurting, you must love until it hurts. Hatred is the human soul's anathema. It is antithetical to everything that Jesus taught and did. In our weakest moments, we have to remember that Jesus told us that what he did, we shall also do and greater. Love ain't for cowards. Love is the province of the bold, the mighty, and the courageous.

I knew that if I relied on verbatim scripture, I would lose Rick and myself. He and I were street people. The ghettos, penitentiary, and the myriad of hardships that navigating those treacherous terrains entail had rendered us cynical and slow to trust.

In that dark, dirty, and depressing hospice ward, weighed down by death, only that which was most sincerely believed could be communicated. To express anything less than what was sincerely and profoundly felt would have been disrespectful and shameful.

"We got it better than Jesus," Rick declared. "He was innocent." I wanted to tell Rick that Christ suffered being human only thirty-three years and that he and I have agonized and suffered much longer, but that seemed blasphemous and inappropriate.

"Yeah, and our living and dying arrangements are much better, too," I agreed.

"We got a TV to watch, a radio to listen to, folks give you dope to help with the pain, and the people who know you ain't saying that they don 't. Hell, they pay me a buck and five a day to keep you company."

"Yeah, 1ife is good," It was nearing four o'c1ock in the morning. I had been with Rick three hours beyond my scheduled four hours. But it was my privilege, honor, and pleasure to be with him every moment. My relief had finally arrived and Rick was visibly tired. He readied himself for bed.

"I'ma trade place with Big-Boy so I can come back tonight and hang out with you if that's cool," I said to Rick as I 1eft the room.

Rick simply offered me a silent and knowing stare, which seemed to say that all we have is now. Tomorrow is not promised to anyone. The present is truly a gift. Appreciate it and maximize its blessing. The time I spent with Rick, that now I had with him will last me forever. In fact, right now, the present moment, is the only thing that's forever.

What time is it? It's always right now. Eckhart Tolle resoundingly answers in *The Power of Now*.

Death surrounds us and serves as life's only true constant. We are told that death and taxes are guaranteed. You can evade taxes; you can cheat on your taxes. But there is no evading death. You can't ever cheat it. Death is given to us all by a merciful, benevolent, and divine source. We don't have to trouble ourselves with a name for that Divine Source. In the prayer offered by Jesus, "Hallowed (Holy) be thou name," Death is Its final gift.

Make peace with death. Invite your end with open arms. Remove all notions of morbidity from death and you'll find life to be exceedingly rich and rewarding. When you no longer fear death, you'll be free to love everyone. You can more easily and courageously give everyone the power to destroy you and the trust not to.

It is our feeble and pointless attachment to life that make us vulnerable. Sophistication demands that we acquire knowledge, power, and prestige. We come to admire those whom are most clever and crafty. Our system of life conditions us to measure love through sex, gifts and quid pro quo. Power is determined by how much influence we can exert on external matters and how much material wealth we can amass. Mankind is left with a fundamental question: Is true power determined by our will to power? Or is it determined by our ability to love?

I have an answer to those questions, but I don't know if my answer is the product of vanity.

As Nietzsche proclaimed, all that is done from love is beyond all good and evil. Of course, Nietzsche might not have meant that love is necessary to overcome good and evil. But I stand by my interpretation of those words.

Chapter II

Junior, Me and Harney

"Stand on ya bet," Jamaican Junior said. "You can't off no bet." You make a bet or choose a path, you are bound to it. If you chose badly, the consequence could be awful. If you renege on a bet, the consequence will be worse than awful.

Life, without a doubt, consistently presents us with options. A sad condition to life, according to Sartré, is that "we are condemned to be free." Humans can always choose, even if we sometimes choose not to choose. That indomitable and indubitable freedom to choose often infuses us with anxiety and other angst. Folks like Junior and me chose the longest and loneliest road on earth to travel, and we knew it.

We both bet that our courage and ingenuity would be enough to get us to our final destiny, safe and sound, whatever that means. You cannot off your bet once the game begins. Honor demands that you keep what you chose with respect to creed.

Junior was older than me by about five or six years. But our ages didn't separate us. Our mutual experiences with the 1980's drug-culture forever united us by our creed and deeds. The predatory world that Junior and I knew only too well insisted that we stand on a belief not grabbed from the heavens or sustained by bent knees. Go hard and be hard. This was our silent mantra.

I believe my dear friend, Junior, would have felt offended if a hospice care worker was assigned to him as he endured his sickness. A person who didn't know Junior would likely perceive his desire to not appear weak as an exercise in machismo. However, he was not masquerading as a tough-guy. Jamaican Junior was the real-deal, genuine tough-guy.

Junior had ruined his kidney by entertaining his appetites for alcohol and cocaine. He hustled hard, realized a degree of ghetto-success, and fiercely indulged himself. It wasn't always easy for Junior to maneuver his way around the manifold machinations launched against him, but he understood that his life choices meant that he would have to face evil with its intrinsic hardships.

When Junior faced evil and hardship, he did not drop to his knees or beg for mercy. Junior didn't believe in some supernatural source of evil. He felt that man was wicked enough on his own. Joseph Conrad was not alone in his secular notion about evil. God or the devil could not be blamed for your predicament. The universe has laws; every effect has a cause. It doesn't matter how good or bad anyone is, the laws of the universe will not be suspended for him or her. Our ultimate predicament will be determined by what we say, think, and do.

If you abused your body with drugs and alcohol, chase women to satisfy your prurient tendencies, neglect your children, and then fail to amass millions of dollars in the process, you could very well end up in the Jessup Regional Hospital, on its hospice ward, alone.

Life has shown Junior and I that your destiny is what you find when you take the road to avoid it. Poverty and degradation showed itself to be Junior's destiny on the ghetto streets of Jamaica. Hence, he avoided those streets only to find himself imprisoned in America, where he remained in dire straits until he died in the hospice ward.

"Why ya sittin' wid tha white-boy?" Junior would ask me when I came on duty to sit with Daniel Harney. "He'd spit on ya grave if he could, ya know. Fuck em!"

My Jamaican friend felt that I demeaned myself by sitting with Daniel Harney, for Harney was a proud member of the Ayran Brotherhood, an unapologetic racist organization. I had had enough arguments with Junior over the many years that I'd known him to know that I could never convince him that it was morally proper that I sit with Harney and provide him with as much love and attention as he would permit me to give.

It wasn't easy for me to sit with Daniel Harney. I was wrongly taught to meet hatred with hatred. Daniel Harney often used racial epithets and bitterly complained about there being too many "dark people" working in the hospital. Harney's soul was being ravaged by hatred and doing more damage to him than the diabetes and cancer.

I am intimately familiar with hopelessness and all the dark thoughts it brings. No one who has ever enjoyed a modicum of dignity and self-respect wants to be pitied. And any warmth given to a dying man in a prison hospice ward will likely spring from pity.

I carried with me the lessons borne from Job's experience. Job's false comforter came to him and in essence told him, "Just die, Job ... you must've done something wrong to offend God."

"Nope," Job said. "Didn't do anything wrong." That story resonated through my conscious in a poignant but subtle way as I worked on the hospice ward.

When my dear friend Drew first came to teach philosophy at the penitentiary, he used the Biblical story of Job as the text to study. More than two decades ago, Drew lovingly and unwittingly challenged me to appreciate eschatology and now invites me to write about it as I face it every day in my job assignment in hospice care.

Forgive me as I digress. When I think or feel that I am coming close to the end, my own eschatology, I just want to slow it down some... What the hell, let my epitaph read, in part: He was loquacious, but equally eloquent. Otherwise, he would have burdened and annoyed his audience. That said, I would often say to Harney, "Why don't you die? Wouldn't it be best for us all?" The narcissist within me sometimes needed to express himself.

Harney's reply would sometimes be to pull out the feeding tube that was inserted into his stomach, get out of bed as quickly and suddenly as he could, and go into the hallway. He would not eat or take his medicine. Harney just wanted to die and not to be pitied.

Harney and I had our moments. He once got himself stuck between the metal railing of the bed. Harney weighed no more than eighty-five pounds at the time. He was emaciated and filthy. No one wanted to touch Harney and he knew that. His five-foot, nine-inch frame was something to look away from.

"Do you want me to help you, Mr. Harney?" I asked as he struggled to get himself untangled.

"Yeah," I could hardly hear Harney's whispered reply.

I didn't put on any protective gloves. I lifted Harney up as gently as I could and put him in bed. The duty nurse joked that Mr. Harney's penis was dangerously close to my face.

I went to the bathroom and washed my hands and face. Harney didn't exercise any hygienic practices, good or bad. He often defecated on himself and laid in it. Harney was hateful and mean and he insisted on being left alone.

When I returned to the hospice ward from the bathroom, Harney motioned for me to come over to his bed so that he could say something to me. I thought that he was going to thank me for rescuing him.

"Tray, you think I don't like you 'cause you black," he said. "That isn't true; I hate Jews. I love black people. I love black people so much, I think everybody should own at least one."

It was hilarious. That was one of the funniest jokes I had ever heard, and it was delivered to me at a time when I needed laughter more than anything.

I wanted to share that joke with Junior, but my friend was the stereotypical Jamaican in one respect: he would argue about anything at any time, and I loved him for it. If I would've told Junior about Harney's joke, he would have given me hell for providing Harney with my service.

I would come out into the hall to see if Junior wanted my company. If the lights were on and he was sitting up, not isolated in his own thoughts and opened for company, I was welcome to come into his room to keep his company. If he was in agony, Junior wanted to be left alone. Unless you genuinely loved Junior, you couldn't possibly know the depth of his pain. He lived like a lone soldier. What the most polished among us would say with their fancy words, Junior would say with his actions. He'd make no apology for who he was. Everything he thought, said, and did were his apologia.

Whenever I lie, I use words to do it. I have never been able to use my actions to lie. Trust me, I have tried and tried, but, my actions will not lie for me. Thus, I claim that I have not grown soft and effeminate. I have grown stronger and better equipped to combat the harsh reality of life in prison.

I seldom give voice to what another person's life meant to me for fear of minimizing others. The fact that I am here and able to communicate these thoughts demonstrate that I was loved and well cared for at important points in my journey. Otherwise, I would not have made it through to the next, and on to now.

Alas, it is a travesty of epic proportion to commit a person to poverty. There is an Ethiopian Proverb that states: Where there's involuntary starvation, all the well fed people are thieves. In a society filled with thieves, it is a triumph in its own right to endure life's cruelest challenge — poverty — and then say, with pride, "You can't break me and cast me among the broken and defeated men. I did it my way, and yes — a resounding yes, I have regrets. But hell, you show me a person who has no regrets, and I'll show you a person who hasn't lived."

Junior and Harney lived life on their own terms. I believe they were foolish in many ways, and they begrudgingly expressed their manifold regrets. But they navigated their way through some of life's roughest terrains — poverty, imprisonment, ignorance, and sickness. When they reached the end of their road, Junior and Harney maintained their convictions and may have been damned for it.

Junior was not going to love or even like someone who hated him. Sometimes my exceedingly argumentative friend would wait until midnight or close to one in the morning, when the hospital was quiet to ask me, "Why ya let that blood clot cracker live? He wanna die now, why don't ya let 'em? Go back to ya cell and go ta sleep."

Any corrections officer or medical staff who dared to ignore Junior's question would be verbally eviscerated. Junior was that Jamaican brother who would argue about anything. Once, when Junior was on the regular tier, before his organs started to shut down, he prepared himself to argue with anyone who found Kevin Hart funny.

We were in the recreation room watching television. There were about fifteen or twenty of us convicts watching a video of Kevin Hart's stand-up routine. It was seven 'o clock in the evening and time for the nightly news. But some of us were still watching Kevin Hart's routine. We did not want to change the channel to watch the news.

"Who thinks he's funny?" Junior questioned. "He ain't funny." No one was going to gainsay Junior. To do so would've resulted in an argument that could last for days.

There were no mean-spirited intentions in Junior. He was simple, self-possessed, and pure. Junior's final days were reflective of his life. He would not be pitied or praised.

Junior would simply be honored because he deserved it. Nothing lofty or ostentatious had to be said about him. Junior didn't seek praise. Honor him in your heart as a good man. Do not speak of his human frailties and weaknesses.

Harney, on the other hand, while he wanted to die and be honored in his death, simply captured my pity. He was such a low-brow person. The medical staff, prison guards, and everyone in the hospital usually awaited my arrival. For when Harney saw me, he would leap out of bed. In a single instance, Harney would cast off atrophy and demand my focus and the entire ward would fall into laughter... because sitting with Mr. Harney was, indeed, an adventure.

I would often come to Harney's bedside to give him some Now & Later candy. That seemed to be his favorite. He would reject Mary Jane candy, but he was a sucker for Tootsie Rolls or any other chocolate. If I was exhausted and didn't feel like dealing with Harney's antics, I would whisper to him something cruel. That usually silenced him - unless it didn't. How can you impose fear upon a dying man? Did I want to? Harney did tell me that he loved me. He felt that everyone should own at least one black person. That's why I offered him pity, something a person awards to an inferior.

I experienced a dilemma that significantly changed me. On the one hand, Junior was quite convincing. It was very humbling, perhaps humiliating, for me to sit with Harney and devote myself to his comfort as he faced his own death. I don't wish to offer a cliché, but the truth is that I didn't know that I had grown spiritually and emotionally as a result of spending time with Harney.

I came to appreciate, after Harney died, that it is easy to love someone who loves you in return. It's easy to care for someone or provide a service to someone who is pleasant and well-mannered. But it requires strength and spiritual maturity to love someone who isn't lovable. It is not easy to provide hospice care to someone who is ill-tempered and base. That is why the patient who presents me with the greatest challenge to care for also presents me with the greatest spiritual and psychological rewards.

Chapter III

Extinction is Different from Death

The time I spent with Hakim, Rick, Harney, and Junior made me realized my worst fear: extinction. Aside from my memory of them and that of a few other family members and friends, who will know that Hakim, Rick, Harney, Junior existed? If they were of any importance, they would not have had to die in a dirty hospice ward. If they were of any significance, some degree of political and social power would have been asserted to give them a more humane and dignified end.

Life shamefully insists that you have to do more than be born human if you want to be treated humanely. This is a dog eat dog world. Each man or woman born is called upon to author his or her own epitaph. If mine were written today, it would read: He died in prison abandoned, alone, and impoverished. Of course, there would be questions if my epitaph was a condemnation upon myself for leading such a contemptible and fruitless life such that no one was inspired or encouraged to love or care for me in my time of desperate need. Or would it mean that I chose my friends and associates badly?

It has been said and demonstrated time and time again that life is a hard-hearted affair. None of us will get out of it unscathed or alive. For death is the stake we all pay in order to live. We come into this world endowed with a number of intrinsically wonderful qualities and abilities. How we nurture and express them will reflect our character or the opportunities given to us.

I came to realize that it is self-defeating to lead a selfish life. A man or woman must come to a point where he or she holds something or someone to be greater than himself or herself. Karma will never be suspended. You can only reap what you sow.

When you plant hatred, greed, and selfishness, expect loneliness, sickness, and destitution. No one, other than the greatest of all fools, will ever teach or declare life to be easy. Life is suffering. It is filled with hardships and difficulties. But each of us possesses divine qualities that are significant enough to make the world easier and more beautiful. There will always be instances where we can return an insult. There seems to be a lot of folks suffering one misery or another. It is easy to assume, "I can't help 'em all. So I won't help anyone." A great number of people let apathy overcome them and, therefore, look at the world with indifference. Thus, a huge gulf has grown between the fortunate and less fortunate.

Some folks motivated by pity may feel encouraged to do some things to relieve the suffering of others when it is convenient. But pity is the product of a superiority complex. And natural laws dictate that things get their power or value from their opposite. For instance, beauty is valuable because of ugliness.

Wealth is given power because of poverty, and superiority is made manifest by inferiority.

If pity is launched at a people, they very well just might assume an inferiority role and collect gifts and become dependent upon alms. Otherwise, the person bestowing the gifts will declare the people ingrates and take his gifts where his supercilious beliefs can be best valued or appreciated.

Just think about how the state issues out welfare checks. If a person is poor and has children, some state governments will give that person a monthly or bi-monthly stipend to pay bills and purchase a few miscellaneous conveniences and will continue the same practice to the next generation as long as none of the recipients of the gratuity upsets the status quo by seeking an education or skill set that'll free him or her from dependency. Governments need to maintain some people in poverty so that it can boast noblesse oblige.

Of course, there are views that are probably less cynical than what I present here. Just as a thing gets its value from its opposite, so do opinions and philosophical notions. When a person is truly open-minded, he can hear the equal value in opposing views. But more often than not, most of us see and hear things with our individual prejudices, which is okay. It would be foolish of us to journey through life without being wisely discriminating in our choices of friendships, schools, clothing, what we devote our time to, etc.

If Hakim, Rick, Harney, and Junior had been more discriminating in choosing their friends, perhaps someone other than fellow lowly prison inmates would have been their comforts when they died. There is no disputing the fact that we are rewarded or punished by virtue of what we think, say, and do.

I am, without a doubt, a Christian. And I'm as proud of the best of my belief system as I'm ashamed of the worst. That said, I do not believe that God operates as some petty despot. He does not punish or reward us because we satisfy a theological tenet or not. God simply gifted us with life and challenges. What we do with the life and challenges that God gives us, is our gift to Him.

God blessed me with a great mind. But I often squander my gifts. That is why I am quick to say that a lot of people can equal or even best my intelligence. But precious few can beat me at being stupid. For instance, I had a wonderful wife. She was a loving, generous woman. When she failed to give me the attention that my all-consuming ego craved, I pointed out all of her flaws and shortcomings. I drove her away and plunged myself into loneliness and isolation.

The zeitgeist does not escape me. We are living in the most challenging of times. Nihilism haunts us to the point that we are beginning to afford very little worth whatsoever to traditional values such as honoring vows and commitments. A large number of people, specifically young people, see the future as doomed or nonexistent. And so, instant pleasure becomes their chief goal in life.

Nihilism compels them to believe that if the future is doomed, why not enjoy themselves now? When I was a counselor for Project Turnaround, a service group committed to deterring youths from a life-style of crime and violence, I attempted to convince this twelve-year-old black boy that using drugs, having unprotected sex, and selling narcotics on street corners would lead to an early death or a lifetime of imprisonment. But he was convinced that he would die before he reached twenty-one. It made absolutely no sense to him to focus his attention or to apply any effort to traditional values such as being respectful to himself and courteous toward others, and getting a good education, so that his potential may be realized for a glorious tomorrow.

He felt no need to respect the laws of society. I concluded from this encounter that hope for the future is lost and must be found or restored if we are to survive as a people.

It pains my heart that we live in a time when you can ask an eight-year-old kid, "What ya gonna be when you grow up?" And the kid may very well reply, "What the hell you talkin' 'bout? I'll probably be dead before I'm sixteen."

We are living in a time when children five, six, seven, and eight years old have a sense of their own mortality. Children in previous generations were sheltered, nurtured, and protected. They had no notion of their own death. You could have presented the question, "What are you going to be when you grow up?" to a poor black child in segregated 1921 Mississippi, and he would have likely said, "When I's all grown up, I'm gonna leave dis place and go on to be a lawyer"(doctor, police, airplane pilot, or fire-fighter).

Previous generations may not have had the wealth or political and social freedom that we have today, but they had hope for a better future. And hope is what separates man from other animals in this world.

If I do not welcome hope into my life and surround myself with folks who feel hopeful about a better tomorrow, I will become extinct. The spirit of the time, the zeitgeist, is frightening. Harmless hedonists have become dangerous heathens. Those who practice wholesome, traditional values such as being respectful and courteous, and pursue an education or skill set to make manifest our fullest potential are looked upon as soft or stupid.

The zeitgeist demands that you exercise discrimination in all that you do because lowly, dirty, and lonely prison wards will not discriminate against you. We cannot ignore the fact that we live in a very competitive world. Our society is predicated upon the principles of capitalism. Thus, there must be winners and losers. It doesn't matter where you start in life: rich, poor, or in between. You have to become a consequential person.

"There is something infinitely better than making a living," Mary McLeod Bethune wisely declared. "It is making a noble life."

More than thirty years ago, when I was a sixteen-year- old boy, I was arrested, charged, convicted, and ultimately sentenced to life plus twenty years in prison for a murder that I did not commit. It is futile for me to claim that I am innocent because I have never been innocent.

I am just not guilty of committing the murder for which I stand convicted and sentenced to life in prison. It would seem that I have every reason to be angry and bitter, but I am not. Providence has allowed me to be who I am. My personal strength of character allows me to do what I need to do, and I am sure that I will get what I want, for I have no doubt that a useless life is an early death.

Of course, I do not fear death. I fear extinction, which will become of me if I do not adhere to the demands of my genius: love the truth and tell it as I see it. Thus, it is incumbent upon me to trust my own experiences, observations, and beliefs. I must not subordinate my experiences, observations, and beliefs to others. If that makes me arrogant and intolerable then so be it. I have paid and will continue to pay what it costs to be me: a meaningful and purposeful man who will be remembered long after I am dead.

Chapter IV

Lesson of Life: Forgiveness

"No man's knowledge can go beyond his experience," John Locke wisely warns me that my views are limited and provincial. The farthest I have ever been from the ghetto streets is the state's penitentiary. My knowledge, if what I know is called that, is parochial and renders me rube. However, I offer it with love and without reservation.

Life's crucible has taught me that forgiveness is intrinsic to spiritual, psychological, and intellectual growth. If a man fails to develop to the point where he can forgive all wrongs committed against him, real or imagined, he will condemn himself to a psychological hell that is fraught with loneliness and fosters bitterness, resentment, and hatred.

I make this averment with an intimate awareness of how cruel man can be towards man. Thomas Paine's eloquent declaration resonates with truth: Man alone is cruel. No animal in God's creation, aside from man, inflicts pain and injury for the sheer pleasure of it.

A number of treacherous acts have been committed against me and I have committed treacherous acts against others. This very competitive material world strongly encourages frequent heinous acts.

"Ain't nobody got time for no broke-ass-nigga," my loving Aunt Kim used to say.

If you wished to be of any worth or significance in this unforgivingly material world, you simply have to find a way to amass some wealth and its accouterments.

There is no dignity and honor in poverty. Poverty offers only hardship, misery, and humiliation. If a man has to abandon all sense of morality and propriety to escape the fiendish clutches of poverty, no one, other than the people he may injure will begrudge him. This is the tacit lesson of a capitalist society.

In order to get from the bottom to the top and stay at the top, we must seemingly inflict harm on one another. The act of forgiveness may portray you as weak if you are a ghetto-dweller destined for the penitentiary. Hell, for me, forgiveness wasn't possible.

Twiggy stood before me with tears welling up in his eyes, the bush-whip toilet sword, a homemade knife, tightly tied into the palm of his hand. I was backed into the cell; there was no way I could escape. "I forgive you, son. You was just a fuckin' baby," he had said. Twiggy was a coward who pulled a knife on me. Zeitgeist demanded that I afford him no expiation.

I was terrified. Twiggy was six foot two, muscular, and a very dark-skinned black man. Twiggy was a convicted serial rapist and murderer. I had killed his younger brother over a drug dispute and Twiggy wanted to kill me. When the time had come, his cold stare excited my primordial fear. And I could never forgive him for holding my fear in his hand and then showing it to me.

There was nowhere for me to run or hide. Twiggy and I were both serving life sentences at the Maryland Penitentiary. Nothing other than air could separate us. My cousin had already provided me with a homemade knife that would rival Twiggy's. But Twiggy had caught me slippin'. I had let my guard down and now excrement was running down my leg.

The humiliation and shame I felt were not assuaged after Twiggy walked away because Bobby, who was my cell-buddy, and World, my home-boy, had come to the cell. They stood in the doorway of the cell where Twiggy had only moments ago stood in the same spot. I was a disgusting sight to see.

How disastrously foolish was Twiggy to ignore the sage advice of Machiavelli? "Any harm you do to a man, do it so thoroughly you need not fear his revenge."

It became my sole focus to settle things with Twiggy. My ego was severely injured. My pride was on the line. I had to prove that I was not just a tough guy out there in free society when I had a gun and associates to aid me. Niggas in the penitentiary had to know that I was a genuine bad-ass.

I was about nineteen years old at the time. I had been in prison for about two years, but my bona-fides had not been established. The first major test to my gangsta had made me shit my pants. I had to rectify matters.

Suffice it to say, Confucius was correct in saying, "Before you embark on the road to vengeance, first dig two graves." Twiggy gave his life to teach me forgiveness. I can hardly close my eyes and not see his gentle face telling me, "I forgive you, son. You was just a fuckin' baby."

The only confession I offer is that the matter of forgiveness presents me with my greatest challenge. It shamelessly reveals my tendency toward hypocrisy. On the one hand, I seek forgiveness for the many wrongs that I committed, while on the other hand, I find it quite difficult or impossible to forgive the wrongs committed against me. I simply convince myself that there are some acts for which there can be no forgiveness.

Oh well, what can be said that is more profound than the French Proverb that states, "There is no pillow so soft as a clear conscience." I cannot reject my belief that confession is a weakness; courageous and wise men keep their secrets and suffer their punishment in silence. Perhaps I speak to the shibboleth here. I would imagine or hope that I do not have to provide a confession or equate confession to forgiveness. For experience has shown me time and time again that when I offer genuine forgiveness for a wrong committed against me, I almost immediately experience a lightness and joy in my heart and soul. Whenever I hold onto contemptuous feelings that result from thinking that I was wronged or treated unjustly, I ache with anger until I exact revenge. I get an uncomfortable tightness in my stomach. My stress level soars and my passions rage out of control when I come into contact with someone I feel has wronged me. My usual ability to reason and maintain a charming countenance disappear. Whenever I interpret an act committed against me to be wrong or some kind of slight, an anger engulfs me that knocks me off my equilibrium. I cannot regain my control until I forgive the person, the people, or the act itself that so angered me. I cannot deny the transformative effect that forgiveness affords me.

But still, I often find it difficult to indiscriminately extend forgiveness. I often wonder if my inclination to hold onto anger makes me a masochist. There are times when someone may wrong me and he doesn't even realize it. It was not the product of malicious intent that did injury to my pride. It was simply my interpretation of the matter that rendered me disturbed. I understand this in an intellectual way.

Long ago, I learned about an ABC system: "A" stands for activating event, "B" stands for belief system, and "C" stands for ,the emotional consequence. B causes or directly leads to C. In short, our belief about an activating event is what causes our emotional consequence, our feelings. For instance, if someone steals my wristwatch, and I become angry about the theft, it is not the stealing of my wristwatch, per se, that has me angry. It is my belief that I own the wristwatch; it is my personal property and no one is supposed to take it without my permission. That belief is what has me angry.

If I were to renounce ownership of all personal property, and declare all the things in my possession a matter of community property, then I would not likely be angered by the theft of anything. My belief system would not allow it.

Alas, I have come to realize that anger, which gives birth to hatred, resentment, and bitterness will eat through and completely destroy any human heart that tries to contain them. We humans are vibratory creatures. We all desire to be accepted, loved, cared for and cared about. But when we allow anger to overwhelm us and infuse us with hatred, resentment, and bitterness, we inadvertently push away from ourselves the things we desire: to be loved and forgiven for all the sins we may have committed.

Chapter V

A True Exercise in Forgiveness

The world's most opprobrious and wretched people prey upon the most vulnerable of the vulnerable - orphaned, impoverished ghetto children. By the time I was nine years old, I had to already know how to deal with child molesters and other sexual deviants. The people that vulnerability and desperation attract.

My fourth grade teacher, Mr. Timothy Michael Martin, at Elmer A. Henderson, Public School 101, was a notorious pedophile. He typically paid young boys a dollar to perform fellatio on them. If Mr. Martin took a special interest in you, he would invite you to his home in some distant place where sodomy occurred - and the material gifts that he bestowed would be substantially greater than a buck. However, your reputation would take a brutal beating and you'd likely walk bowlegged for a while.

It was rumored that Mr. Martin sometimes made his prey cry. If you were not aggressive with Mr. Martin, he would be aggressive with you. For instance, when Mr. Martin would attempt to kiss me, I would spit on him or hit him as hard as I could in his stomach or his groin.

Each time Mr. Martin performed fellatio on me, he never seemed to have a whole dollar for me, as he did for the other boys. I complained to my best-friend, Squirt, who had introduced me to Mr. Martin and acquainted me with his sexual predilection. Squirt had told me that Mr. Martin was always good for a dollar.

"Squirt, every time that faggy-ass Mr. Martin suck my dick, he be tellin' me he ain't got nothin' but seventy-five or eighty cents," I told him.

Squirt and I were walking home from school, and I was showing him the three quarters I had just received from Mr. Martin.

"Yo, you can't be goin' for that shit!" Squirt was adamant. "You betta start pattin' that punk's pockets when he give you short ends."

I had been with Mr. Martin on three different occasions: once in the classroom after a school day had ended, once in the boys' bathroom, and once in his car when he was taking me home after I had stayed after school to clean up the classroom.

We all knew that what we were doing was wrong. It was nasty, but tolerable if I did not allow myself to be "bunned in-the-butt." Squirt and I knew that Mr. Martin was bunnin' Chris because Chris was weak. He was timid; therefore, a punk like Mr. Martin could make him into a faggy.

Of course, the only person I would openly talk to about my relationship with Mr. Martin was Squirt. He was in Mr. Martin's fourth grade class, a year ahead of me. It was his duty, as my best friend and hustling buddy, to turn me on to where the money sources were. Mr. Martin did not mess with any student who was no longer in his class. Therefore, I would not be infringing on Squirt's money source.

When our notice had come to inform us which teacher we would have at the start of the school year, I told Squirt that I would be getting his former teacher, Mr. Martin.

"Yo, you got Mr. Martin," Squirt quipped excitedly. "If he go fo' you, he'll give you money to suck your dick every day."

I was quite familiar with all the rumors concerning Mr.

Martin as well as all of other perverts situated in our community. There were a number of ministers, teachers, and various other adults who enjoyed sexual relationships with us children. Sometimes it was homosexual and sometimes it was heterosexual. The zeitgeist held that if you were old enough to know about it, you were old enough to do it.

If a girl was sexually mistreated, she could tell someone, go to the police. But a boy could never report being sexually abused. To the black male in the ghetto streets, "Tellin' is for the weak and ignoble. The courageous must forever maintain his silence and endure the punishment to his soul."

It was my ex-wife, Francine, who persuaded me to unburden myself and report Mr. Martin to the officials. She and I were engaged in one of our very private and intimate conversations. She was telling me all of her shameful and painful secrets, and I told her mine.

Francine could not believe that I had been in prison for more than fifteen years, close to two decades, and had not had a single homosexual encounter or relationship.

"Tray, come on now," Francine had grudgingly insisted, "You ain't never been with another man after bein' locked up for sixteen years?"

"No," I believe a sadness manifested itself that only a shameful secret could force into fruition.

Francine was quiet, tender and completely accepting. She allowed for me to tell something that I had not told anyone, except Squirt, in more than two decades.

"When I was nine, in the fourth grade," I started giving voice to my abuse, "There was this teacher named Mr. Martin..."

I paused. I felt a tear welling up in my eye because I felt a sense of guilt and shame. My relationship with Mr. Martin had always left me feeling derogated and humiliated. But Francine persuaded me with her love and acceptance that the shame belonged to Mr. Martin and not me.

I continued, "He used to pay me a dollar to suck my dick," I laughed a nervous laugh. But Francine remained serious and quiet. "Seriously, he used to offer me a dollar to suck my dick, but every time he did it, he'd only give me seventy-five or eighty cents."

I went on to explain to Francine that the experience was quite painful to me physically, perhaps because I was not old enough to ejaculate, and it disturbed me emotionally. Everything in my upbringing condemned male homosexuality.

"You shall not lie with a male as with a woman," dictated Leviticus 18:22.

"You have to report this to the police," Francine decided.

"You know that ain't gonna happen," I was in a state prison serving a life sentence for murder. My gangsta bona-fides were well established. There was no way I was going to sacrifice my credibility by snitchin' on a faggot. I did not tell on my criminal associates, which would have freed me from a life term of imprisonment. How could I possibly start tellin' now?

"The hurt you feelin' right now, baby," Francine was gentle, "How many more children he got feelin' that way?"

I would not easily relent. It took Francine's monomaniacal persistence to convince me to snitch. She would not discuss anything with me aside from reporting Mr. Martin. She went as far as to withhold intimacy from me.

"You comin' to the function?" I asked my then wife.

"Nope."

"You ain't gonna give me no pussy?" I was in a panic. Mr. Martin wasn't that important to me. He would have to go to jail.

Francine compelled me to acquiesce; she made the necessary phone calls and told a Sergeant Forester from the Maryland State Police everything that happened between Mr. Timothy Michael Martin and me. The detective visited me at Roxbury Correctional Institution in 2001 or 2002, and I told him about three other boys with whom I knew for a fact that Mr. Martin had had sexual encounters with.

When appropriate, I now tell others about my experience with Mr. Martin because I realize that my experience with a child molester was not peculiar or unique to me. It is quite common. However, boys are not permitted to "tell on" their abuser in the same way that girls are permitted. We suffer the shame in silence and take our soul through a needless torture.

I was a nine-year-old child. Mr. Martin was my fourth grade, adult, teacher. The shame is his and not mine.

I have not sought professional counseling to aid with the emotions I felt or was supposed to feel. My sense of humor comforts me and I find satisfaction in knowing that no burden will be placed on me greater than I can bear. Moreover, I have come to accept that in life, you must learn to laugh at the things which would ordinarily make you cry. Otherwise, you'll be considered weak.

Squirt told me that Mr. Martin was testing me when he would offer me a dollar only to give me seventy-five or eighty cents. Thus, I was to aggressively go into his pocket and take what I was owed. If I behaved meekly with Mr. Martin, I no doubt would have been "bunned-in-the-butt." I probably would not have been able to forgive Mr. Martin had he sodomized me - as I was told he sometimes did to other boys.

When I think about us boys, who experienced Mr. Martin, how we became drug-addicts, murderers, and miscreants of every sort, I wonder just how much of an influence he had on my decisions. Prior to meeting Mr. Martin, I was taught how to be aggressive. I possessed the knowledge and capacity to deal with the likes of a pedophile by the time I was nine years old. That is a very telling statement in and of itself. We live in a world that is so vicious and cruel that children are not allowed innocence.

The most loving responsible parents and guardians of ghetto children must prepare their children for a fallen world. When a child is still a baby, if he is a ghetto child, he must become skilled in maneuvering himself around the most fiendish of predators. If the child does that, then the grave-yard or penitentiary awaits him. No ghetto-child can escape the toll of a fallen world.

Dostoyevsky wrote in *Crime and Punishment*, "The degree of civilization in a society can be judged by entering the prisons." I venture to say that the degree of civilization is better measured by honestly observing how a society prepares its most vulnerable citizens for prison.

I am truly grateful that the universe has given me the capacity to forgive wrongs inflicted upon me. For I am not strong enough to bear the burden of hatred.

Mr. Martin wronged me in the most fundamental way imaginable. Tears were necessary to forgive him. Through tears I learned that tears are not a sign of weakness. Tears are merely a message from the soul to give voice to unspeakable pain and hurt.

I have been told that a man who can keep a secret is wise, but he ain't nearly as wise as the man who has no secret to keep. What became of Mr. Martin, I don't know. If he is alive or dead is of no consequence to me. I don't have to kill my enemies or inflict any form of violence upon them to be victorious. If I outshine them and stand brilliantly in the harm they caused me, I win.

I have been imprisoned for more than three decades. My closest and dearest friends and family are gone. I contend with an abysmal emptiness and loneliness. But I do not hide behind any illusions. The environment that produced me and nurtured me and provided me with the strength I would need to navigate the vicious and unforgiving world that was thrust upon me condemns me to an existence that I find abominable.

No self-respecting man can live as a prisoner in perpetuity. While I have forgiven those who have wronged me, I also forgive myself for the wrongs that I have committed. Hence, it is time for me to enjoy freedom.

A number of friends tell me that I deserve a second chance at life, as if I had a first chance. But those friends will not undergird that support with anything aside from words. I lead a very frustrating existence. I have not been able to achieve my desire to live a life. My world constantly reminds me of the fact that death is universal because everyone dies. But not everyone gets to live.

Chapter VI

The World is Hostile to Those Who Don't Know the Rules

It is not possible for me to think about death and forgiveness without remembering Avery. He was a dude I met at the Maryland Diagnosis Center prior to me going into the penitentiary. Avery was an exceedingly affable fellow. He stood at about six feet even, with smooth brown skin and a pretty smile. It is without doubt that Avery was good-looking, but not as good-looking as me.

I could not fathom why Avery would rape women. He was good looking and charming. But he was a convicted rapist sentenced to life in prison. Perhaps Avery was innocent of what he was convicted and sentenced for. Who cares? The world is a cold and unforgiving place. Moreover, it is hostile toward those who don't know the rules.

"Tray, would you like to play a game of Pinochle?" Avery would politely ask.

"Fuck yeah," I would often reply. "Why not?"

Avery kept a brand new deck of cards, and he prided himself on teaching me how to play Pinochle.

I, in turn, tried to convince him to harden his demeanor. Avery's diction was too precise; his subjects and verbs always agreed. And, he was too damn polite and agreeable to survive the crucible that was the Maryland Penitentiary.

It is difficult for me to characterize my relationship with Avery as a friendship. He and I simply gravitated toward each other while at the Diagnosis Center as we awaited bed-space at the penitentiary. Most inmates at the Diagnosis Center were there for about two to three weeks. Inmates sentenced to life terms of imprisonment or the equivalent numerical sentence of life typically stayed at Diagnosis Center for six months to a year. Bed-space did not become available as quickly at the penitentiary as it did in other prisons throughout the state. For the penitentiary's population was stagnant. Many of the occupants at the penitentiary stayed there until they died.

Avery and I would often look out the Diagnosis Center's massive Plexiglas windows from our sixth-floor perch into the penitentiary's yard. When violent incidents erupted, we would see prison guards hurrying about and, on many occasions, ambulances were summoned.

"Yo, there goes one," I would deadpan.

"Maybe that'll free up some bed-space for you and I," Avery usually offered.

At every possible opportunity, I warned Avery that his gentle demeanor and polite manner would be a disservice to him. But Avery insisted that I was young and simply hadn't experienced enough of the world to understand.

"You'll catch more flies with honey than with vinegar," Avery once said to me.

I told him, "In that pen, your honey gonna catch ya dat dick."

Why did I tolerate Avery? I shall never know. The only thing we had in common, aside from our shared humanity, was our blackness. Avery was twenty-six or twenty-seven years old; clearly a decade older than me. He was reared in a stable, two-parent, suburban home. Avery graduated from college and had had a career, I, on the other hand, was an orphan. I was illiterate, knew nothing of stability and pursued only violence and criminality.

Fate would have it that Avery and I would be called for transfer from the Diagnosis Center on the very same day. The time had finally come to leave the sky-scraper penal institution in downtown Baltimore that could easily pass for a commercial office building. Avery and I were headed to the adjacent prison. The huge Gothic structure that was built in the early nineteenth century, when slave-owning Thomas Jefferson was the President of the United States.

The Maryland Penitentiary was a menacing place. Any sensible person would pause to summon all the violent strength he could muster to endure the venture. Avery was not sensible. He did not pause to make the necessary adjustments.

When we entered the bull-pen at the Diagnosis Center to be strip-searched and shackled so that we could board the prison bus, there was already another prisoner there. He sat quietly on the bench, obviously in his own private and impenetrable thoughts.

"Hello, how are you?" Avery's polite greeting was met with a harsh stare.

I only nodded my head at the guy.

I did not want to risk revealing what I was feeling or thinking. My broken home, street struggles, and stay at juvenile institutions had prepared me for the moment. I was about to enter the place where, as Dante wrote, "He who enters must abandon all hope."

We were stripped naked. Once we were permitted to put our clothes back on, we were handcuffed, shackled, crammed into a prison bus, and transported across the street to the Maryland Penitentiary. Avery chattered on incessantly. He told the prison guards that he had found the Lord, Jesus, and God would protect him. He professed his innocence and insisted that he would soon be vindicated because his family had connections and they believed in him.

I remember wishing that Avery would shut up. Of course, I could not tell him to be silent because the code, the ethics of the time, demanded that I maintain my own silence. It was only through your speech that your character could be assessed and measured. The men who awaited our arrival at the penitentiary could only determine the degree of our respective strengths and weaknesses by our voices, what we say. Therefore, it was best to say nothing.

When we entered the penitentiary's courtyard at about two in the afternoon, the bright sun was high in the sky and a million pairs of eyes seemed to be glued to us. The prisoner that accompanied Avery and I simply walked along the path the guards had established for us. He did not turn around to look at anyone or anything. He indicated no sense of curiosity.

I assumed a very similar cool poise. Avery did the complete opposite. He spoke to strangers and behaved like some kind of square-ass-tourist.

The inside of the penitentiary stood in complete contrast with the sunny outside. It was uncannily dim inside. The windows were open; there were no curtains to block out the sunlight. But the sun's brightness could not light the prison's interior. Shadows paraded on the walls. They looked like ghosts, not friendly or hostile.

"Take the shackles off 'em," the order came from someone behind us.

We were seated on a wooden bench, and the prison guards who transported us to the penitentiary unshackled us. We remained seated in the prison's property room for about ten minutes when three high ranking officials entered the area. Two of the three were in uniform and from the two bars that adorned their collars, I could see that they were captains. The one in plain clothes, a simple white dress shirt, a tie, and brown slacks identified himself as Chief of Security, Saunders.

Chief Saunders had a slight, but undeniably Jamaican accent. He was of average height and build. There was nothing remarkable or distinctive about him except that he spoke with tremendous authority.

"You were given rules books at Diagnosis?" The chief inquired.

"Yes," came Avery's obsequious reply.

"Yeah," the third prisoner and I answered in unison.

The chief instructed us to go to the box that contained our respective, pitiful personal property, and retrieve the rule book that was issued to us at the Diagnosis Center. One of the captains took the three rule books and casually tossed them into the trash.

"In my prison, there are only three rules," the chief said. "Stay the fuck away from my walls, keep your hands off my officers, and don't ever fuck up my count."

The chief left the property area and the fat white captain followed on his heel. The other captain, a slim, very dark-skinned man with a clip-board in his hand looked at me and said, "Arlando Jones, you're in B-218," He moved on to Avery, "You're in B-326, and Donnell Robinson, you're in C-205."

No one told us how to find the cells we were assigned. We picked up our boxes and left. Once outside, Donnell acknowledged my presence in a friendly manner for the first time, "You be easy, shorty."

Donnell Robinson was hard. The streets had removed all of his naiveté. I guessed that Donnell's age had to be at about twenty or twenty-one, roughly a few years older than me. He was muscular and stood a few inches above six feet. He had light brown skin and was highly self-possessed. Donnell's demeanor was that of a drug-dealer, who had no qualms with violence. In time, he and I would become friends. Avery would become a demon that would haunt my conscience, invade my dreams, and makes me regret the day we ever met.

I located B-218 easily enough. Avery and I had to go in the same direction. Donnell had to exit the main building to find the C-Building.

I had not taken two steps on the tier before I heard Marty Q's familiar voice, "Tray, what's up, boy?"

My two home-boys, Bobby Washington and Marty Q shared cell B-205. Marvin Jay and World, my two other homeys were in cell B-211. We were all from east Baltimore and we knew each other well.

"What cell you in?" Bobby Washington asked.

"Two eighteen."

Bobby yelled down to World, "They puttin' Tray in two eighteen."

There was a brief pause before I heard World's voice, "With the faggy boy?"

It seemed like everyone found that amusing. I would have to share a confined space with a homosexual. This was my welcome to the penitentiary.

I stopped at World's cell in route to my own, "Yo, you bullshittin'?" It had been two years or so since World and I had last seen each other, but the love was still there.

"Yeah, homey," World answered "I'm just fuckin' with you. That nigga just a fuck-boy."

I was left to wonder whether or not World's answer to my query was a bon mot or if there was actually a difference between a fuck-boy and a homosexual. It required an enormous amount of self-restraint not to ask. But I understood that asking stupid questions or making comments could get me into more trouble than doing something foolish. Besides, nature hates secrets. That's why all things are ultimately revealed.

"When we come out?" was all I felt was appropriate to ask.

"When they open the doors, muthafucka," Marvin Jay entered himself into the exchange.

"Word," I accepted the inevitable and went to the cell I was assigned. My cell-buddy, Wallace had heard the exchange between my homies and I, but he did not offer a defense for himself or dare contradict World. He just said that World or

Bobby Washington would probably have me moved to another cell later that night or the next day.

It was beyond my comprehension that this dark, solid man was taking it up the ass. I had entered a world that was upside down and only two wrongs could make something right.

I fixed my bunk and asked, "Why you don't got no TV or radio in this muthafucka?" The cell was immaculately clean, but rather empty. Wallace had very few private belongings, but he had scores of books. They lined the shelves where I thought a TV or radio should have been.

"I don't watch TV," Wallace replied. "I read a lot and sometimes I might borrow my friend's radio."

Damn, Wallace employed that same precise diction as Avery. That let me know that Wallace was soft and unsuitable for the cold and unforgiving penitentiary. I looked into Wallace's eyes and saw that he had already been beaten and defeated by life. The religious books he had been reading were to help him bend his knees so that he might be able to bear the weight of the world.

In the coming days, I received a true prison orientation. I was set and ready for any challenge that would come my way. I was provided with a Butch-Switch toilet sword. It was fashioned from the finest and strongest steel that could be extracted from a cell's plumbing unit to make a knife. Even though my cousin, who was my co-defendant, and an assortment of my home-boys, were at the penitentiary with me, I had to stand on my own two feet. Hell, my closest ally would abuse me if I showed any signs of weakness. The rules were the rules and the creed was always held. The penitentiary was a jungle where the strong must feed off the weak. If you were a beast, you could not deny yourself a feast.

More than half of the Maryland Penitentiary was made up of sexual predators. A cursory glance at the public record would show that eighty-five percent of the men sentenced to life at the Maryland Penitentiary in 1986, which was the year I entered, were convicted rapists or murdering rapists. Very few of them endeavored to temper their nasty tendencies.

"What's up, Avery?" A week or two had passed since I last saw him. It was an open secret that Humphrey, Avery's cell-buddy, had raped him. I had heard the unmistakable sound of him being sodomized in the cell above mine the night it had happened. It was in the late hours of the night. I was lying in my bunk, listening to oldies love songs. I heard the scuffing in one of the cells above me, followed by the eerie, painful sound of a man being raped.

Old Humphrey had turned another one out with his famous "I love Jesus, too" routine. Avery had the look of the broken and defeated on his face. His joyful smile was gone.

"I'm just sitting here, chillin'," he offered a forlorn reply. Avery had to know that I knew. But like all fuck-boys, he protected himself by pretending that no one knew, other than he and his rapist.

It was typical of Humphrey and other predators to integrate themselves into someone's life if they perceived them to be weak and soft. The Bible and religion were the common texts.

Humphrey had convinced Avery that he, too, was a devout Christian. After a few days of Bible-reading and praying, Humphrey offered Avery some homemade wine laced with sleeping pills. Once Avery was in his intoxicated state, Humphrey tied him down and sodomized him.

Hours later, after Humphrey was satisfied, he untied Avery. He professed his sorrow and confessed that he had fallen in love with Avery the moment he stepped into the cell. He told Avery that had he expressed his true feelings for him, Avery would have been frightened away. But now that they had made love, they were united as one. Humphrey swore that he would tell no one. It would be he and Avery's secret alone.

That was all bullshit. The rule in such an instant gave Avery twenty-four to forty-eight hours to kill Humphrey. Otherwise, the entire prison would know that he was a fuck-boy. He was lower on the prison's hierarchy than a homosexual. A homosexual took it up the ass because he wanted it. It was not forced upon him, as is the case with a fuck-boy.

Alas, Avery proved to be the worst of the fuck-boys. Humphrey was able to pass him on in trade to other sexual predators. Avery became the subject of the most ignoble discussions. I felt humiliated and ashamed to know him.

"Ah, Tray, what's up, home-boy?" Avery greeted me in the G Building one evening.

"Punk-ass fuck-boy," I snapped. "I ain't your muthafuckin' home-boy."

My response to Avery's greeting was venomous and shameful. From the moment Avery and I first met, he had been good to me. He freely shared his commissary with me when I had nothing. He shared his scholarship with me by helping me write intelligent letters to the court, my attorney, and my girlfriend.

Marty Q, World, Buddy-Clyde, and all of my other east Baltimore home boys laughed at Avery as he hung his head in shame and left the G-Building without even trying to use the telephone, play ping-pong, or participate in any of the activities that were available to us in the G-Building. I was too hard-hearted at that time to give Avery a second thought.

Two days later, World came down to my cell as I was preparing to go to the dining hall for lunch to tell me, "Your punk-ass home-boy in the cell hangin'."

It did not quite dawn on me what World had said at first, "Hangin?"

"Yeah, nigga. Avery up 'dar in the cell dead," World cleared up my confusion. "He hung it up."

World was known for being callous. Still, I had to see for myself. I went upstairs to Avery's cell, and there he was, hanging from the vent above the sink and toilet.

A brown extension cord was knotted around his neck. He had on a pair of dark blue jeans, a white T-shirt, and white socks. His brown eyes seemed to protrude from their sockets. They stared at me, accusingly, condemning me for betrayal. I was likely the only friend that Avery had had in the entire penitentiary and I had turned my back on him because he did not have the knowledge of life to be able to navigate the low and savage world of the state's penitentiary.

Over thirty years have passed, and I still see Avery hanging there with the waste dripping down his leg, staring at me and accusing me of not being his friend after he had been mine. All I can do is offer up a feeble ass, "I'm sorry, Avery. Please forgive me, 'cause I can't forgive myself for how I treated you."

Chapter VII

Death Can Be A Friend

Long before I became acquainted with Dostoevsky's *Notes from The Underground*, World had taught me that it was foolish to live beyond forty.

"Avery couldn't do it no more, huh?" World asked me later that evening on the same day Avery had hanged himself.

I was sitting on my top bunk trying to wrap my head around all of the ugliness and death that characterized my world. I figured my behavior could have been described as morose. I was profoundly disturbed by Avery's death. I didn't know what it meant to me. It was, indeed, of great significance to me and it should not have been.

Avery was just another nigga I had met in the joint. I was already familiar with how sudden death could occur. I was an orphan child who had navigated Baltimore's streets amid poverty, drug addiction, violence and other sorts of devastation. By all account, I was a villain. It was unsettling, to me, that a weak-ass rapist, who committed suicide, was causing me emotional trouble.

"That nigga ain't a fuck-boy no more, huh?" I countered World's question with one of my own.

World stepped into the cell, searched through my collection of cassette tapes, selected Whodini, and put it into my radio. *Friends* began to play and World began to praise Avery's courage.

"I ain't think that nigga had the heart," World started.

I interrupted, "It don't take no fuckin' heart to kill yourself."

"Yo, you soft like most these other muthafuckas 'round here...," World was saying. "When you can't wake up with a woman beside you, eat what you want when you want it, go where you wanna go and live like a man is supposed to live, you should have the heart to kill your fuckin'-self."

World's words had struck a nerve with me. They resonated with my soul and rendered me silent. I had no response other than to defend my character.

"I ain't soft, muthafucka."

World offered a wry smile, took my Whodini tape from its player, selected two or three more of my tapes, and left. He didn't bother to ask if he could borrow them. He knew that he had provided me with invaluable wisdom. Something worth much more than my favorite tapes: Whodini, Stevie Wonder, and Anita Baker.

When the news reached me, which was a little more than a decade later, that World had hanged himself while in a segregation unit at the Maryland House of Correction's Annex, I smiled that same wry smile in honor of my courageous friend. He finally ended the farce we call life.

Life can only be lived when you have the liberty to pursue your happiness. A prisoner, like a slave, can only dream about a life. Life, as World said, in the most apropos manner, is when you can wake up with a woman beside you. Life is being able to eat what you want to eat and go where you want to go whenever you want to go. Life means standing up like a man and enjoying the fruits of your labor.

If you have to crawl on your knees and beg for alms, mercy, and forgiveness you're existing as a slave, as a prisoner. Men walk upright with courage and dignity. Men engage their liberties to pursue happiness and prosperity. It is every human being's inalienable right to choose the path that will give him satisfaction. And if existence, as we know it, fails to offer any meaningful opportunity for satisfaction, one is free to kill himself.

Jean-Paul Sartre offered ineffable wisdom when he declared that "Man is condemned to be free," in his essay, Existentialism is a Humanism: Of all the animals God created, man is the only one who doesn't have to be a slave to his instincts. Man can always choose. He can even choose to kill himself. And that freedom to choose is the primary source of man's anxiety and panic. For instance, when a lion is hungry, he has to hunt and eat. A man can fast for spiritual reasons or diet. If a dog is in heat, she has to mate. Humans can delay or await sexual activity, mating, until their romantic interest is at its peak.

A prisoner's world is wrought with challenges and each one is seemingly designed to render a prisoner broken and defeated and incapable of living a meaningful life. We are put on a very regulated schedule. We eat breakfast, lunch and dinner at pretty much the same times each day. The times at which we can be visited by family and friends are equally regulated. A prisoner, in many respects, is a child. He is being conditioned and shaped.

It requires revolutionary thinking, and sometimes behaving, for a prisoner to break free from the bondage of submission and servitude. The prison system cannot operate efficiently without passiveness and docility on the part of the prisoners. If prisoners insisted on being men and pursuing happiness and prosperity, the prison system would collapse.

Avery and World used their freedom to choose a path that I am far too cowardly to even consider. Many of the folks I admire died long before they reached the age of forty. The criminals, the dope-fiends, and the downtrodden thrown into prisons, these were the members of the world that I know all too well and they typically struggled through the misery until one of life's happenstances killed them. My wit gets me past the typical hardships that kill off many of the others. Combine my foolishness with my wit and I'll likely live until I am ninety or so.

If I navigate prison properly (and what I mean is get out of prison), I will prove to World that I am not soft. I have tolerated all the miseries, hardships and humiliations that come from a life in prison simply because I was convinced that I would be made strong by it all. If I felt that prison would break me and defeat me, I would employ my inalienable right to choose death. What exists in between life and death is the pursuit.

In the pursuit of happiness and prosperity, we might, as hedonists oft do, mistake pleasure for happiness. But happiness involves so much more than pleasure.

In fact, pleasure is usually accompanied by pain. Since time immemorial, man has unsuccessfully attempted to separate the two. Thus, the wise accept that if you pursue pleasure, you are also pursuing pain.

Prison is populated by unwise hedonists who inflict pain in the pursuit of their pleasure. If you are not built to be brutish or, alternatively, built to shield yourself from barbarous acts launched against you, prison will reduce you to a "life" of servitude and submission. Once a man in prison allows himself to be reduced to servitude and submission, suicide will become too noble an end for him. This is why I am conflicted about Avery's death.

When I juxtapose World's suicidal death to Avery's, I easily conclude that World behaved nobly and Avery did not. World looked forward and saw an environment that would not allow him to be a man of honor and dignity. He wouldn't cling on to life until he was broken and defeated. Avery gave himself up to servitude and submission. Death, even with its unknowns, was more appealing than living on as Avery would have. Hell, death was the better option for both Avery and World. It's just that one died broken and defeated, and the other abandoned life before that fate could befall him.

In my experience, I often wonder if death, even suicide, would be better than this. There is no honor in existing as a prisoner. We are hopelessly dependent upon the support and generosity of others for our survival. We are locked in tiny cells which, for the most part, we share with another. A prisoner's life is monotonous and tedious. The only way a man with a sense of honor can endure prison is if he someday hopes to be free.

I suspect that of all the animals God created, none requires more space than man requires to live. We remove creatures from the jungles because we need more space for our recreation and resorts. When you observe man exploring the heights of the heavens in outer space, he is declaring that the earth is not big enough. It is therefore easy to conclude that man requires more space than what any prison could provide.

Each day that I spend in prison tortures my soul and wears me down. I rely heavily on that mystical promise that holds that "God won't place a burden on you, greater than you can bear." Moreover, I accept that God chastises those He loves the most. It is that belief that persuades me to hold on. It propels me forward into a new future.

I know all too well the hopelessness that haunts the days and nights of a prisoner. Death takes on the role of a welcoming and comforting friend. He screams out, "Don't wait for me. Come to me, now!"

My arrogance then answers back, "I'll see ya when I see ya. I ain't gonna run to ya. I'm here and I'm not afraid of you as I once was." The *Tibetan Book of The Dead* taught me that until I befriend Death, I can never really appreciate life. Hence, I lie when I tell you that I run away from death. There are moments when I search for death. That is disturbingly easy for me because everything around me dehumanizes me almost in an effort to make death look appealing.

I attend religious worship and study classes where no one comes close to protesting against the daily wrongs and injustices that we, prisoners, face here in the Maryland prison system each day. Our religious leaders preach different versions of acceptance. Prison "life" is unadulterated decadence. How could death be worse than this? We have lost human rights and privileges that were fought for and won.

Each day that I endure this modern prison, I feel that I am experiencing torture to my very soul. How does the soldiers' adage go? **A coward dies a thousand deaths, a soldier — once.**

That question makes me wonder if Avery was a soldier or not. He died by suicide just as World had, a man that I know was a true soldier. Avery died each time he was forced to behave as a subservient prisoner among prisoners. World died just that once.

Alas, I am well-acquainted with death. I have befriended It, perhaps. That is probably why I had to quit my job assignment as a hospice care/observation aide worker. Broken and defeated — or maybe, just misguided prisoners too often pretend to be under psychological distress. They threaten suicide, and I am then summoned to sit with them for hours. These defeated prisoners are no closer to committing suicide than Frankenstein was to finding genuine love and acceptance. They treat suicide, death as if it is a toy.

Of course, that is perfectly okay. Death should not be taken too seriously. It just annoys me, personally, I suppose, that inmates whom I characterize as cowards would toy with death. They mimic it out of ignorance.

It is unfair of me to judge a number of the folks in prison simply because they do not value death. How blessed are those of us who know that life can only be fulfilling for those who welcome death as a comforting friend. Those who fear death will inevitably be filled with anxiety. The mystery that death shrouds itself in frightens the common man.

There is a reason why there is more prey than predators. There can only be one emperor at a time. A common element shared by predatory creatures is that they all recognize death. They accept that all things must come to an end; therefore, they dare to write their own eschatology.

It is a well-established fact that most individuals will go to greater length to avoid what they most fear than to achieve what they most desire. How many of us desire to reach the peak of a mighty mountain, but the fear of height prevents us from even contemplating the attempt? Death has too many unknowns for our comfort. But worst of all, we cannot kill death as we have other things that we perceive to be indomitable.

Death's prevalence can only be appreciated by the warriors' class. The weakest among us see death as this dark abyss; a depth to be avoided at all costs. The notion that it's best to "die standing on your feet than to live crawling on your knees" repulses the coward and weak. The quantity of a life span is of greater value than the quality of a life span to the weak and lowly.

The mean ghetto streets and treacherous penitentiary tiers that forged me into the loving, honorable man that I am today threatens to render me extinct. Just as evolutionary matters wrought the dinosaur into the biggest and meanest predators on earth at one point, its unawareness or inability to adjust to the zeitgeist rendered it extinct. The dinosaur failed to do what the atmosphere demanded.

Renowned French philosopher Michel Foucault tells us that in order for the modern prison to work, the inmate population must be made docile. I was placed in a prison that was built when Thomas Jefferson was in office. The Gothic structure situated in downtown Baltimore reeked of violence. In order to live there, you had to assume your role as either predator or prey. The penitentiary did not allow for neutrality.

I chose to be a predator. If you were in the role of the prey, you subjected yourself to a lifetime of submission, a fate that is arguably worse than slavery. I insisted on developing an intellect that would allow me to be a creative thinker so that I would not have to be told what to think, as prey are conditioned to do. I insisted, as I navigated the penitentiary, just as I had navigated the ghetto streets, that I be better than my circumstances. For that reason, the prison zeitgeist, with its insistence on making the prison population docile, threatens my existence.

There is not a single life event void of the wonderful possibility for reward. When the human soul acquaints itself with death, it befriends It. There will be no challenge terrifying enough to defeat such a force. God created a kingdom for all His creatures. It is up to you and I alike to pick up your crown and wear it, as Oprah so eloquently stated. For in this world, you'll either rule or be ruled. You will define who you are, or you will be defined by someone else. It all comes down to what lens you see life through. There is only one certainty to living life as a prisoner: a prisoner will forever be confused. The prisoner who believes he is not perplexed is the most confused of all. He must resolve every existential matter there is to settle. Paradoxical issues must stand as sheer balderdash.

Mother Teresa saying that "If you're hurting, love until it hurts and everything else will disappear except the love" is bullshit to a prisoner. A prisoner hurts - period. The very purpose of prisons is to punish its inhabitants and to make them feel subhuman because they offended society. In order for prisoners to enjoy human rights and privileges once again, they must constantly fight for them. If a prisoner becomes docile and accepts servitude and submission as his nature, death will be his only comfort. No words can be used to explain the purposeless and meaningless existence of a prisoner.

I embraced the notion long ago that it is best to live one day as a lion than a thousand years as a sheep. It is nonsensical to argue against the reasoning of those who prefer the longevity of a sheep to the brief life of a lion. The cowardly sheep conceptualizes differently than the courageous lion, just as quantum physicists and mechanical physicists do. In that same vain, it is difficult to the point of impossibility for me to explain to a person who isn't a prisoner what the life of a prisoner is like. (But I must try. I am a fool, remember that!)

How can I possibly use words to clarify why World's suicide was noble and Avery's suicide was not? Any action made by a pusillanimous man in prison is deemed ignoble unless proven otherwise. People in free society are free to see life in all its different hues. Prisoners are condemned to an exceedingly narrow world-view. We embrace prejudices that limit our moral and intellectual development, or we don't. "In prison, things are what they are and will forever be." That's that. Oscar Wilde asserted that truth an eon ago. I take on a herculean task trying to explain prison to non-prisoners, for living and dying differs from the free persons and prisoners. Only compassion and patience can bridge the gap. For what human, aside from a prisoner, can possibly know what it's like to exist as a nonhuman?

Chapter VIII

Here Comes the Leder

1993 proved to be climacteric for me. I was invited to see things in the many shades of gray. Everything was not simply black and white, predator or prey, or win or lose. There is a root to everything, but there are many paths to the root of all things.

That likely makes sense only to those of us acquainted with phenomenology, that branch of philosophy that compels one to look beyond appearances. For nothing is what it appears. Of course, that sounds cynical, which is okay. It is a phenomenologist's duty to be cynical, or at least appear to be cynical, even if he does not admit it.

I am likely to forever remember when I met Dr. Drew Leder. It was the beginning of summer. I was on semester break and I had just completed my junior year at Coppin State College. I was too smart to know how dumb I was. I was infatuated by my own intellectualism. The more eloquently it presented itself to me, the more persuaded I was to mistake it for wisdom.

"My name is Drew Leder," this skinny-ass white dude with a long nose and unruly brown hair began. "I am an associate professor of philosophy at Loyola College in Baltimore."

Drew went on to tell us why he wished to introduce us to college or graduate level philosophy. He was funny and humble in his delivery. I was absolutely amazed by Drew's curriculum vitae. He had a fuckin' Medical Degree from Yale and a Ph.D. from Stony Brook University.

"You can call me Dr. Leder," he had said. "Or you can call me Dr. Square."

I couldn't help but interrupt, "What about square-ass-doctor?"

Drew laughed a genuine laugh and we all settled on calling him Drew, even though there was never any doubt that he was the leading intellectual in the room and deserving of the title "Dr. Leder."

The course was supposed to last through the summer. Only college students or those who had graduated college could attend. There was a standard to be maintained. The remedial effort needed to prepare the less sophisticated in the penitentiary would have likely taken away from our group.

We were about to acquaint ourselves with the accumulated wisdom of the ages via the most stellar conversations imaginable. The ninety days of summer were not nearly enough time to do it. The course went on for eighteen months without interruption. We seemingly went to every era in time and examined a myriad of religions, cultures, and ethnic groups, and mysteries. In that tiny prison, in a secluded, dimly lit classroom, living under draconian conditions, we studied the phenomena associated with space and time through Bollnow's, Hegel's, and Heidegger's perspectives. Thanks to Heidegger, Bollnow and Drew, I became aware as to why I experienced certain positive and negative sensations in some spaces and why time seemingly moved quickly or slowly.

Simone Weil, Nietzsche, Cornel West, Thomas Moore, Joseph Campbell, Martin Buber, Malcolm X and many other phenomenal thinkers challenged us to explore our morals and judgments. Socrates, Plato and Aristotle merely whetted our appetite for knowledge. This was not some common pedagogical experiment. In fact, we came to regard the traditional pedagogical approach to teaching oppressive, tedious and unproductive. We discovered that learning through elevated dialogue, a didactic method, was far more rewarding.

At the beginning, a segment of our class felt that Drew was intending to westernize us to our collective detriment. The war on crime was fresh, and white America, via subterfuge, was advancing the miseducation of black folks. If we black people did not wish to remain downtrodden and mistreated in perpetuity, we had to look to Afro-centric principles for guidance.

If Drew was going to carry us to new places and introduce us to perspectives different from our own, we had to carry him to new places and introduce him to alien concepts.

The Raphael, Zen, and "Too Black and Too Strong" elements of the class encouraged us to go to Africa's history and stolen legacy. They declared that we will find that European, western philosophy was literally stolen from Africa and white-washed.

There was a cornucopia of information presented. Drew brought in this couple, the husband, an African professor who was an expert on African History and Mythology whose wife was white. She came to our class on a separate occasion, and demonstrated an equal or greater understanding of Africa's religions, customs, and history. For the two to three weeks in which Drew's colleagues led the lectures, Drew became a fellow student. We were humbled and exalted by our newfound understanding of Afro-centricity.

The segment of our class led by Raphael was determined to prove that Drew was some white man operating as some kind of villainous agent sent to advance the "miseducation" of black people. The pseudo-scholarship presented by Raphael and his group of seven or eight was thoroughly, but respectfully, debunked.

Before the summer concluded and the regular school period began, Raphael and company left. Our group had dwindled down to thirteen or fourteen. It was great; we were the crème de la crème, the elite members of the Maryland Penitentiary's intelligentsia.

Drew found funding to purchase books for our intimate group, and in that tiny classroom, nestled away in the back of the school building at the state's penitentiary, we traveled to every place on earth. There were even times when we had to use our imaginations to go to outer-space to better appreciate the knowledge we were developing. One time was especially challenging because we agreed to use the literary work of Fascist-sympathizing Martin Heidegger, Being and Time, to try to grasp a better understanding of space and time.

It was during that time that I came to realize that words, concepts, ideas and deeds rooted in love and compassion cannot be restricted by boundaries or physical borders. In fact, profound ideas are the greatest of all monuments. Cathedrals and other lofty buildings are restricted to a place and time, but ideas expand beyond place and time and extend throughout the millennia. Cathedrals cannot do that.

The philosophies and ideas developed in ancient China found their way to us in Drew's philosophy class. We demystified the *Tao Te Ching* and made Confucius simple. We were quickly becoming custodians of esoteric information.

We explored western notions of power and morality. We compared them to eastern thoughts and were challenged to define what was just and honorable in our own hearts and minds. In the mist of hell, surrounded by death in an environment plagued by violence and overwhelmed with darkness, we resurrected hope. I, personally, achieved the highest form of sanctity: while living in hell, I found hope.

Prior to meeting Drew, getting to know him, and loving him, I thought that the greatest teachers provided their students with ample information to advance their scholarship or personal interest. I now know that the greatest teachers do not teach a damn thing. They simply create an atmosphere that allows for the greatest learning.

Once the fledgling revolutionaries departed from our class, we were down to thirteen or fourteen undergraduate and graduate level students. We were then better equipped to grasp this wisdom. It was not easy, but always fun. Some personal animosities manifested themselves. We approached matters of race, religion, power, sex, and culture. No subject was too sensitive for us to openly discuss.

I felt a special animosity toward one of my fellow classmates, a guy named Mr. Skinny (H.B.). He was pretentious and rotten inside. H B. had AIDS. When he came to the penitentiary in 1985, he knew that he had that deadly disease and yet, he shared needles with a number of other intravenous addicts. He intentionally infected them. That in itself could never be excused. I could hardly stomach his expressions of love for the community as if he felt a sense of nobleness. Drew would allow this man to ramble on about one philosophical tenet or another and it grated my senses. I had to tolerate H.B.'s hypocrisy because social niceties demanded that I hold my tongue and not give voice to the actual contempt that I felt for him.

Brother John and Donald, my closest friends and allies in the class, knew how I felt about H.B. They strongly encouraged me to leave penitentiary matters in the yard or the tier. I can recall a conversation I had with Donald about H.B.

"Duck, I swear wid everything I got," I had said shortly after a class session, "I hate that rottin' muthafucka."

I was certain that H.B. had intentionally infected my fellow prisoners with the virus that causes AIDS. "All them dudes 'round here shootin' dope together, Tray," Donald exercised patience in explaining to me what I already accepted to be true. "If you shootin' dope, sharing needles, and fuckin' faggies, you gonna catch AIDS and die."

My cousin and the multitude of others that may or may not have been infected by H.B. seemingly forgave him or did not care one way or another. H.B. was living his life and desperately trying to get out of prison before he died. He had full blown AIDS. His once caramel-colored skin was now ashy. He was nearly six feet tall, but he was often bent over from his illness and appeared much shorter. His thinning gray hair spoke volumes.

"Skinny ain't gonna be long in this world," Brother John had told me "Let him do him."

I wanted to tell Drew that H.B. was a false alarm, but nothing within the code of prison ethics would permit me. Drew was not some naïve child. Besides, as a philosopher trained in phenomenology, he should have been able to see beyond appearances. Drew was likely the person with the most compassionate heart that H.B. would ever know. Who was I to interfere?

It was important that we all develop a sense of camaraderie for our class's success and advancement. We had something special going on and that much was undeniable. However, we did not all like each other. It is not possible to deposit thirteen murderers, rapists and fiendish hoodlums of various types in a single room and expect that there would be no animosity. Drew's genius was rooted in his dedication to philosophy. That was the sole reason for our class's success.

When anger would launch a vicious attack upon me, the class's structure insisted that I delay my response. Therefore, I learned that delay is an adequate and most effective response to anger. Our time in ancient Greece had already revealed to us the proverb that holds: **Before the gods destroy a man, they first make him angry.**

Of course, anger was an emotion I knew all too well. It was consuming me. I was eight years into a life sentence and entering my senior year at Coppin State College. For the first time in my life, I had the power to choose between something positive and all the negative shit inside that penitentiary

Initially, it did not seem like Drew was providing me and the others with a life line. The philosophy class was simply a course to take during the hot summer months to pass the time away. No degree of prescience could have let me know that Drew would remain in my life for more than a quarter century and still counting. When we discussed the matter of a secret relationship existing between Jews and Blacks, I assumed that

that was some conspiracy theory concocted by wicked bigots. But perhaps there is a secret relationship between Jews and Blacks. I openly love Drew and I am truly grateful to him for creating an atmosphere that allowed for me to grow morally and intellectually and to acquaint myself with wisdom.

I have been in prison for well over three decades. Aside from Drew's presence in my life, everything in my biography would strongly suggest that I remain a simple man at best. But philosophy has enabled me to demonstrate that I can be better than what my life circumstances prescribe.

In *Man's Search for Meaning*, Dr. Viktor Frankl emphatically declares that once a man discovers why he lives, he can easily figure out how to live. Under conditions that I panic to even imagine, Dr. Frankl discovered a purpose for living.

The Nazis were plotting to kill every Jewish man, woman, and child. In Hilter's Germany, every single Jew was made superfluous. Dr. Frankl survived because he found meaning and purpose in life, and he challenges everyone else to do the same. Drew, a Jewish man, encouraged us all to find meaning and purpose in our own lives. Through honest dialogue, a bridge was built in our class and the most ignorant among us were lovingly, and often humorously, invited to cross over and come into wisdom.

Chapter IX

Appreciate the Warning

"Go easy on Nietzsche," Drew warned me a time or two. I have a fascination with Nietzsche. I believe he is among the wisest men to have ever lived. His wisdom is what probably drove him mad.

I found Nietzsche's declaration, "God is dead" spoken by the madman in *Thus Spoke Zarathustra* to be the principal ingredient when it comes to all wisdom. Of course, Nietzsche is often misunderstood. It is quite difficult, if not impossible, to accurately interpret him.

What can I say? It takes a madman to truly understand a madman. I, too, am mad. That is why I understand Nietzsche in a peculiar way. My life's circumstances demand that I be mad. When Nietzsche declared that "God is dead," he was telling us that the incomprehensible and infinite God that created the entire world and everything in it was too baffling for man. Therefore, we rid ourselves of that God, the Creator of all things, and created a god - through our various philosophies, ideologies, and religiosities - that we could restrict to our limited imagination.

Mankind murdered that which stood outside of the finite - the infinite. If we cannot measure it through science or reduce its existence into something that fits comfortably into our religious understanding, it must die or be cast into oblivion, which is hosted by the abyss, the eternal darkness.

I have gone into the abyss, met up with oblivion, and wrestled with darkness. It drove me mad, but strengthened me enough to accept the God that created all that exists and stands beyond all comprehension. That was essential to acquainting myself with the accumulated wisdom of the ages — accepted and recognized the God that is beyond comprehension.

The *Tao Te Ching* tells us, "... Naming is the origin of all particular things ...." I am one with God and inseparable from Him/Her/It. I refuse to be labeled or named by others. Once I accept a label, I am reduced and rendered less than magnificent.

Nietzsche constantly tells his readers to be magnificent. That message resonates with me, but puts me at loggerhead with prison officials. Prison authorities label me an "inmate." The comfortable and confining definition of an "inmate" is a convicted felon trained to be docile and accepting of whatever privileges and liberties he is allowed.

I repudiate the name "inmate." Moreover, it is a taxing and exhausting chore to sit among folks who embrace the label. When a man permits another man to name him, he is not qualified to offer me his opinion or view on anything.

Genteel society produced Drew; therefore, when Nietzsche warns us to be careful when fighting monsters, lest you become a monster yourself, he likely interprets that very differently than

I do. While Drew and I lived in the same hell, navigating a fallen world, we fight different demons.

"When you look into the abyss," Nietzsche provides. "The abyss looks into you."

Only a small percentage of the penitentiary's population attended school or involved themselves with academics. Hence, Drew's access to our world was very limited and so was his understanding of what forged our psyche.

In Drew's philosophy class, inmates who were reduced to nothingness in the dark and savage abyss of the penitentiary were elevated to a human status. We were students, intellectuals and fellow human beings in Drew's class. If I wanted to be a part of the class, I had to be compassionate, patient and tolerant of others as our teacher was. Of course, Drew did not teach us in the traditional pedagogical way to be compassionate, patient and tolerant. He simply embodied those characteristics and invited us to embrace them.

"Fuck-boy burn me up when he be talkin' that strong black man shit," I whispered to Brother John.

"Don't start!" Brother John was not interested in this kind of conversation.

Silly-Boy was speaking. Drew had given him the floor to talk. It irritated me to listen to Silly-Boy. He represented everything that I believed to be shameful. A man named General, a charismatic sociopath, had persuaded Silly-Boy that he would impregnate him.

General was the leader of a fringe Black nationalist group, Organization for African-American Unity (O.A.A.U.). Silly-Boy was obviously the lowest member within the group's hierarchy, for the members of the group routinely sodomized him at General's urging. The purpose for sodomizing Silly-Boy was to get him into the *Guinness Book of Records* as the first male impregnated.

It was generally known that General had wagered that he could convince Silly-Boy that he could get his life sentence overturned if he got him pregnant. Silly-Boy was gullible enough to believe it. And so, he submitted himself to fuck-boy status.

The penitentiary was the most wicked place on earth. General, just to name one of the many sociopaths who inhabited the prison, was warning enough as to how monsters must be fought. Submission to General, or to anyone of his kind, would be to the detriment of your psyche. The milieu of the penitentiary was designed to either destroy souls or improve them. No one who entered the penitentiary could go untouched.

I have come to realize, albeit, begrudgingly, that those who were beaten and broken by the penitentiary are equally deserving of respect, patience and tolerance. I am not superior to those who fell prey to the penitentiary's myriad of predators. In fact, I show an inferiority by demonstrating a bad temper toward them.

Yes, I was changing in a rather drastic way. Philosophy was having a meaningful impact on me. Our classes in advanced philosophy were scheduled for once, sometimes twice, a week. But the materials or subjects that we were studying required thought that occupied much of my day. We were studying Martin Buber's "Where art thou" theme. Genesis tells the story where Adam and Eve are in the Garden of Eden. They are told that they may freely eat the fruit from every tree except one. "... But of the tree of knowledge of good and evil you shall not eat, for on the day that you eat of it you shall surely die."

I was coming to the conclusion that God's question of "Where art thou?" was a perennial question designed to transcend time and space. That most profound question was not just for Adam and Eve to answer in the Garden of Eden. "Where are you?" comes to each of us from God. We are challenged to contemplate that question every day of our respective lives.

Eve and Adam ate from the forbidden tree. Once they obtained knowledge of good and evil, they were cast from the safety and security of God's garden. The question was now squarely before me: Tray, where are you?

My answer was resounding: I was in a terrible place emotionally, spiritually and physically. I was fucked up. I was filled with bitterness, resentment and hatred. I understood the world to be fallen and broken. I knew love from only a peripheral perspective. I was far more knowledgeable of hate. There was little to no doubt in my mind that all human actions were motivated by either love or hate.

Hate motivated most of my actions because it seemed to induce fear. I had lived a relatively lavish lifestyle because I inspired fear. The fear that I inspired kept me from becoming one of the penitentiary's pitiful fuckboys. I could not imbue myself with love because that would not have been in my best interest.

"Let me holla at you, Tray," Chim-Chim had stopped me as I was on my way from B-Block.

It was a Monday and I was running late for my philosophy class. "What up, Chim?" I asked. "I gotta get outta here before they start the count."

"Fuck the count," Chim-Chim wrapped his arms around me and brought me in for an embrace. "I'm goin' back to Supermax, homie."

I had books under my arms, so I could only offer one hand to Chim-Chim as we separated. "What the fuck you talkin' 'bout, man?" I looked into Chim-Chim's brown eyes and saw that he was serious. "This 'bout your short-man complex?"

Chim-Chim flashed me a strange grin; the man never smiled. Chim-Chim believed that men who smiled in the penitentiary were weak, or it was indicative of a paraphilia. He was a mere five feet, six inches tall and beginning to show signs of having AIDS.

Chim-Chim was still muscular in build, but his hair was starting to thin and his once smooth and dark skin looked ashy like H.B.'s did.

"Ya man, Mark disrespected me," Chim-Chim launched a bold indictment. "Whore-ass nigga called me outta my name."

It was not that serious; had he called Chim-Chim a "bitch" or a "fuck-boy", Mark and Chim-Chim would have likely fought on the spot. "Let me holla at ya 'bout this latta," it was nearly three o'clock in the afternoon. If I did not get out of the building, I would be locked in the wing and not allowed into Drew's class.

"See him before I do," were Chim-Chim's last words to me.

I had made it to class without a minute to spare. We were about an hour and a half to two hours into the session when Officer Roe White came into our class and announced that there was an emergency situation in progress. The prison was on a temporary lock-down.

This was not the first time one of our class sessions was interrupted because something had gone amiss in the penitentiary. We all started saying our respective "good-byes" or "see you later" to Drew.

"What's goin' on, Roe?" I had asked.

"Somebody got killed in the west wing," Officer White answered.

I did not have to ask any more questions after that. I knew that either Mark or Chim-Chim was dead. A simple stabbing incident that claimed no fatalities was not enough to lock down the penitentiary. Fights and stabbings were a common, if not daily, occurrence.

I was anxious to learn who had died. I considered them both friends. I was not going to tell anyone about the conversation I had had with Chim-Chim prior to arriving to class. In my heart, I knew that I could have stopped Chim-Chim from confronting Mark about whatever it was that had transpired between them. He and I had been in the Supermax together. Hell, Chim-Chim was from my neighborhood. We sold drugs from the same package, spent time together at the Maryland Training School for Boys, and shared a considerable amount of time together on one segregation unit or another. We were very close.

Mark and I had met in the penitentiary. He was a fellow ghetto-superstar. Also, he and I had several acquaintances in common and were familiar with each other prior to coming to the penitentiary. I felt a terrible sense of guilt and shame about not interfering in the matter when I had the chance.

I was getting soft. Death did not always disturb me. It should not have disturbed me then, but it did. I was becoming humane.

"Who got got?" I asked Tee, my cell-buddy.

"Mark, that nigga with the gold fronts," Tee seemed annoyed by the whole sordid affair. "Your fucked up, dope-fiend-ass home-boy, Chim, hit 'em in the jugular."

My curiosity was satisfied. Tee was my man. We shared a lot of secrets with one another, but I was not going to tell him about my conversation with Chim-Chim. Confession is for the weak. A man keeps his secrets and suffers from their torture in silence.

"That ole diseased muthafucka was probably hatin' on that man," Tee was rambling on about why Chim-Chim had probably murdered Mark. "Early today his AIDS-carryin' ass was tryin' to beg for a bag of smack."

I had tuned Tee out completely. My soul was trying to tell me that I was hurting. Tears would soon start to fall from my eyes, but Tee did not love me enough to know that my tears were not a sign of weakness. My tears were simply a message from my soul to let me know that I was experiencing unspeakable grief.

I took off my shoes and laid down on my bunk. I pretended that I was exhausted. I was on the top bunk and Tee was on the bottom. He would not get up; my cry would be a private affair.

Mark's life sentence ended two years after it begun. I imagined him laying naked on a stainless-steel slab in a cold morgue. His soul was free and warm in God's smoothing embrace. Chim-Chim, on the other hand, was likely in some furnace-hot cell in the Supermax. His body and mind would suffer through the effects of AIDS. Chim-Chim would not experience a loving human touch. He would likely pray that death hurry up.

I was lying on my side, facing the wall. My tears were drying, and my vision came back into focus. A Helen Keller quote, likely put on the wall by some other prisoner who had once occupied my bunk, was neatly written, in perfect cursive, before me:

The best and most beautiful thing can't be seen or touched, but felt with the heart.

It was official, I was mad - just like Nietzsche. The only difference was that I did not have to reduce the God that created all that exists to a comprehensible entity. My world was already embarrassingly small, and my understanding of matters was provincial at best. I had committed a number of wrongdoings and a number of wrongdoings had been committed against me. Life's tendency to be unfair was no mystery to me. It was not designed to be fair. In order for there to be winners, there must be losers.

Where was I? I most certainly was not winning. I was twenty-six years old and imprisoned. Aside from my undeniable good looks, I had nothing. My ability to inspire fear was dwindling. The state's willingness to punish me was having an effect on me.

I grew up in a Christian household. I have heard a lot of talk about love. It was the essence of Jesus' teachings and the very opposite of everything that I believed and practiced. Hatred, the product of fear, brought me greater material gain than love. That love bullshit demanded that I constantly give.

I was experiencing an imbroglio; a divine invitation was given to me to come into wisdom. It would make itself known to me in a most meaningful way. But the invitation came with a caveat.

"For in much wisdom is much grief,
And he who increases knowledge increases sorrow"
(Ecclesiastes 1: 18).

Where art thou? The question echoed within me. I would have to be compassionate and understanding in my judgments. I would have to abandon my propensity to be a hypocrite, which meant that I would have to measure everything, including myself, with the same ruler. The path of the wise is not an easy one; it is a rough terrain. In fact, wisdom is so unruly and unpredictable that it breaks off into many paths. There is no straight road to wisdom. It is often described as the longest, loneliest road in existence.

Ignorance's path is smooth and blissful. It is riddled with fools to comfort one another. There is nothing challenging about ignorance's path and no one cares where it leads. Common folks journey through it and everyone knows that it will take them to common places. Fools make haste to ignorance's path, but the wise never go there. The wise, filled with compassion and understanding, simply look upon the ignorant, on his path to ruin, and wish him well.

Chapter X

My Journey to Proper Loving

The Maryland Penitentiary was in the process of going from a maximum-security prison to a minimum-security prison. It was time for me to be transferred to Hagerstown. My security level was reduced from maximum to medium. I was about to experience a cataclysmic change.

Prison officials informed us that all of the personal property that we wished to take must be able to fit into three cardboard boxes. Anything we had that could not fit into those boxes would be considered excess property and would be destroyed if we did not have anywhere to mail it at our own expense.

When I had entered the penitentiary a decade prior, it had been impressed upon me that I would either die there or be released by the court. I was an exclusionary prisoner. I was not like the vast majority of convicted persons that would eventually be released from prison. I was among the rare. I was not expected to transition through the penal system as a common inmate. When the classification team reduced my security status in order for me to move to a lesser security prison, I felt a little optimistic. I would go on a long drive to Hagerstown, Maryland where I would meet different people and live in a far less crowded environment.

My property was searched and packaged away in the three boxes I was allotted. I was strip-searched, handcuffed, shackled and placed on a huge blue prison bus with twenty-two other prisoners. We were all going to the prisons in Hagerstown. I was going to Roxbury with six others and the rest were going to the Old Jail (Maryland Correctional Institution Hagerstown) and the New Jail (Maryland Correctional Training Center).

All the transportation corrections officers were black. They were quite casual with communicating to us just how radically different our new living situation would be from the lifestyle we had come to know at the penitentiary.

"Them red-necks in the mountain be on some different shit," one of the officers had said. "Y'all ain't gonna be runnin' 'round and gettin' functions. Watch!"

There was endless chatter about the horror stories of racial tension in Hagerstown. "Yeah, they still got niggas buried around Hagerstown in unmarked graves."

If you had a feud going on with Hagerstown officials while imprisoned there, it was best if you had loved ones in your life inquiring about your well-being. I cannot count the times I heard, "Niggas go missin' in dem mountains."

The moment I entered Roxbury Correctional Institution, I knew my stay there was going to be rough. A picture of a nude white toddler bent forward at the waist was featured prominently on the wall to indicate to us new arrivals how we were to position ourselves for a strip-search. There were six or seven of us prisoners in the room with about four or five officers. We were not afforded any privacy whatsoever.

"I'm not gonna bend over and open my ass for you or nobody else," I boldly announced.

"You gonna do it," the belligerent red-neck officer countered. "One way or another."

"I'll do it the other way," I was adamant.

It left me somewhat flabbergasted, witnessing my fellow prisoners from the penitentiary undress, stand in the middle of the room, bend forward at the waist and open their ass to be inspected.

Man-Man and Mark urged me to comply with the officers. They reminded me that we were no longer at the penitentiary. But I would not give in to their entreaty. These murderers and rapists would not resist or protest against a profound insult to their dignity.

"You niggas a bunch of bitches," I did not bother to conceal the utter contempt I felt for those inmates who had accompanied me to Roxbury.

I was ordered to put my hands behind my back. I was handcuffed and escorted to Housing Unit Five, the prison's segregation unit. One of the two officers informed me that I would not be receiving any of my personal property until I complied with the strip-search. There was nothing more to discuss. I was placed into an isolation cell and given absolutely nothing: no washcloths, toothpaste, toothbrush or soap. I was kept in an isolation cell for about forty-eight hours before a lieutenant came to talk to me.

There was nothing peculiar about this lieutenant. He was of average height and build, five foot nine or ten inches tall. He weighed somewhere between 190 and 200 pounds. He was well groomed and stood fully erect as if he was in the military.

"Mr. Jones," I heard the authoritative voice. "Come to the door," the white man with the chestnut hair and cold brown eyes commanded. "You're down here for refusing a search."

"No, I didn't refuse a search," I replied. "I simply refused to stand up in the middle of a room full of people and spread my ass."

I sensed that the lieutenant understood; however, he could not let on that he agreed with me. The strip-search procedure at Roxbury was humiliating and inhumane.

"Listen. Don't speak; just listen!" the lieutenant offered an ominous warning. "When my officers tell you to do something, do it."

I did not bother to respond. The defiant look on my face should have let him know that I am among the least tractable of the whole prison population. The lieutenant concluded by saying, "I'm gonna take you out of isolation, let you take a shower, and go get your property."

The lieutenant left; ten or fifteen minutes lapsed before an officer came to the cell to give me a bar of soap, toothpaste, toothbrush, wash-cloth, towel and a set of underclothes. The cell door was opened, and I was directed to the shower. I brushed my teeth, showered and afterward felt renewed.

I was ultimately given a clean burgundy prison jumpsuit and was told to go to property to retrieve my personal belongings and receive instructions from there about where I would be housed. Once outside in the summertime daylight without handcuffs and shackles, I was able to view the prison complex from a different perspective. It was shamefully beautiful. The prison looked more like a college campus than a prison. There were shrubbery, small trees and little gardens in front of the housing units. The grounds were well-kept. There was a multitude of prisoners going to and from various places.

I recall asking a fellow prisoner, "Where's property?"

He pointed to a distant building and said, "The administration building where you came in at."

I wanted to cut the travel time in half to the administration building by walking on the grass, but then I remembered hearing time and time again, "Those white folks don't play 'bout their grass. Don't ever walk on it." I noticed that all the inmates stayed on the concrete walkway as they went. Only the corrections officers were standing on the grass or inside the neat security booths situated around the compound.

I recognized a few familiar faces and wanted to talk to some people, but was discouraged from meandering on the prison's compound or giving the appearance of loitering.

It did not take long for me to realize that the prison population in Hagerstown was docile compared to that at the penitentiary.

Once I entered the administration building, the officer at the front desk directed me to the property area. I withheld my anger when the property officer took my hot sauce, black jeans, and other items.

"You can't have these in this institution," the officer had informed me with a polite authority. "Do you wanna mail them home or would you like for us to destroy them?"

My wife, Francine, was frugal. She would have lectured me on the evils of being wasteful had I directed the officer to destroy my belongings. Once my personal property was inspected and inventoried, it was determined what I could keep and what I had to send home. The latter was boxed and weighed on a UPS scale. I was informed that it would cost me $32 to ship my belongings to the address I provided. Every impulse within me wanted to tell the officer, "Fuck that box; destroy that shit." **I was serving life. I had no home. My life demanded that I have nothing. Death and all things associated with eschatology loomed over me.**

I was an orphaned, imprisoned and an unapologetic hedonist. Experience and intuition had already revealed to me that I should cling to nothing, not even life. My genius rested on recognizing and appreciating the moment for what it represented. I had no time other than now. That was what I owned. If I concentrated too much on the past, I would feel debilitating anger. There was only loss, betrayal, debauchery and abandonment in my past. The moments of happiness and pleasure that I had experienced were brief and transient. And what future could I possibly have? I was sentenced to prison for the balance of my natural life. There was absolutely no one I knew who was prepared or motivated enough to make the necessary sacrifices to help me best the mighty state.

My wife loved me in her own special way, but she was the typical woman who married a man in prison. Francine was psychologically damaged. She had exceedingly low self-esteem. She would provide me with every comfort she could to help me in prison, but she would do very little to help bring me home. Women like Francine feel valued and secure with their man incarcerated. They fear that when he returns to society, he will leave her for a prettier woman or mistreat her in some unspeakable way.

The future, for me, was bleak. It was a source of anxiety and frustration. The only gift God had for me was there in the moment. I could not receive anything from God unless I seized it right then and there.

I was less than a year into my marriage; propriety dictated that I send what I could not have at Roxbury to Francine. I signed the necessary document to permit the institution to deduct the $32 from my account to execute the mailing.

My personal property was placed into a yellow wheel-cart by an inmate working there.

"Take him to four-A," the officer instructed.

The inmate was a rather short white guy, about five foot six. His brown hair was styled in a short crew cut like some kind of soldier.

"Let's roll, homes," he commanded. I followed him out of the property room. We were both silent until we exited the administration building. Once outside and under the bright sunlight, the inmate finally introduced himself, "I'm Mike."

"And knowing that helps me?" I said.

"It could," Mike was no square. His obsequious facade was simply that, a facade. "If you want it, I probably got it."

"My man," Propriety forbade me from asking him, specifically, what he had. I was not going to tell Mike about the half ounce of marijuana secreted away in my cigarettes. "What's up with four?"

"It's a regular housing unit," Mike informed me. "They got that new antenna system in down there. Y'all can watch the movies and get the channels without havin' to put wires out the window. Plus, all the girls down there. "

Damn, how could Mike believe that I would be interested in homosexuals? Did I look like I did?

I saw a number of familiar faces. Everyone seemed subdued; there was no yelling on the compound or out the windows. I was thrown aback. I had been in the penitentiary for well over a decade and my impression of prison was that of bedlam. Roxbury made absolutely no sense to me. The lawns were manicured. There were small trees in front of each housing unit. I saw two blue U.S. Postal Mailboxes and no cell bars. The vast majority of the inmate population was black, like me. But every corrections officer was white.

It took me about ten minutes to walk from the administration building to housing unit four. The corrections officer at the desk directed me to a cell that was upstairs on a two-level tier.

There were a few inmates on the tier. Two were using the telephones, others were in the shower, and some were standing near the washing machines and dryers. The recreation room door was opened and a skinny black teenaged kid came out. "I'm Dee-Bo," he said to me as he extended his hand for me to shake. "I'm your celly."

I instantly liked Dee-Bo. He was me ten years earlier. "Let me get this stuff in the cell, young," I replied as I accepted the handshake.

Without hesitation Dee-Bo lifted the front end of the cart as I lifted the back and we carried it up the steps. We put all my property in the cell and I returned the wheel-cart to the administration building. I relished the walk; it had been years since I was able to travel such a distance alone. When I came back to housing unit four, it was time to lock in. I could not go into the recreation area to talk to fellow prisoners to better orient myself with the institution. Experience had shown me that the rules written in the regulation booklets issued to an inmate upon his arrival at a penal institution did very little to acquaint him with all the things he needed to know.

Dee-Bo was sitting on the top bunk when I entered the cell. “You can have the bottom bunk, Unc,” He told me, paying homage to geriatrics.

“Young,” I felt an abiding compulsion to say, “I can probably get up and down on that top bunk faster and easier than you.” I was not quite thirty years old yet.

Dee-Bo and I exchanged some light banter. He was reared in Washington, D.C. while I was from Baltimore City. If you reached the age of thirty in the world that we hailed from, you were considered an elder. Chronological years had very little to do with becoming old. One’s experience dictated whether or not you were. I had navigated poverty, crime, violence, betrayal and treachery; my reputation was good. I had not been raped in the penitentiary, meaning that I was no one’s servant. Dee-Bo knew that about me.

“Niggas told me you a soldier from outta the pen,” Dee-Bo said at one point during our conversation.

“Who on the tier from the pen?”

“A couple dudes,” he answered. “Tata, Ralph Alexander, Ole Man Ty. You’ll see ‘em when we come out.”

“When is that?”

“We go eat at five o’clock,” Dee-Bo offered me a glance at the schedule. “When we come back, we lock in for ‘bout fifteen or twenty minutes, and then we go out to the rec-hall. So, by ‘bout six or six thirty.”

We had about three hours before the dinner would be called. I had enough time to clean the cell and organize my property. It was apparent to me from the moment I first entered the cell that Dee-Bo was not among the most interested in hygiene. While he was seemingly well-groomed and slim, I detected he gave little to no concern about cleaning the cell, flossing his teeth, and doing the little things that made for good habits.

I asked Dee-Bo if he had any cell cleaning supplies and, to my surprise, he had plenty.

"How you live," I started, "says everything about you."

I noticed in an instant that Dee-Bo felt embarrassed about the condition of the cell. "That white -boy that was in here with me was filthy," he launched as his defense. "I wasn't gonna be in here cleanin' up behind him like I was his bitch."

"Don't ever let nobody bring you down, shorty," I lectured. I went on to explain to Dee-Bo that he is to never permit anyone to force him to live under conditions that reflect poorly on him. A lot of people enter into the penal system. A good amount of them are dirty. Some were actually hoboes in free society and will dedicate no time or attention to their hygiene. Poor living conditions are of no consequence to them. I told Dee-Bo that it was his sole responsibility to maintain his dignity and self-respect and to become a man worthy of honor.

It thrilled me that Dee-Bo seemed to treasure my every word. He was eighteen years old and had been incarcerated for less than a year. He did not tell me the details of his crime; he just told me that he was serving thirty years for an armed robbery and assault. The cynic in me told me that this young fella was a tree-jumper. My new friend was likely a rapist. He was too desperate for me to like him and hold him in the esteem that he held me. What the hell? Some of my best friends were the worst of all the sexual predators.

The universe was giving me an opportunity to live up to my highest ideals. I had often boasted that I would someday present largesse to my community. **I will be better to the world than the world was to me.** Wherever I go or whomever I find myself with will be made better because I was there.

Dee-Bo could not possibly compete with me. I would easily love him more than he could love me. I recognized his soul - or guiding daemon (as Jungian author James Hillman might phrase it) in an instant. When you understand a person more than he understands you, you are compelled to love him more than he can love you.

Life's burden grows heavier and heavier for those of us who make love the highest priority as Jesus Christ did. It was my fortune or misfortune, it depends upon one's perception, to endure the crucible of the ghetto streets and then the penitentiary's tiers. I witnessed human beings give into their most primordial instincts. What I personally experienced lends credence to Joseph Conrad's declaration: **The belief in a supernatural source of evil is not necessary; men alone are quite capable of every wickedness.**

I would serve as Dee-Bo's big brother, uncle, or teacher in order to help him become a better person. The best way to serve Dee-Bo was to first love him. I vowed to myself that I would operate from my highest level of understanding when I related to him. I would guard my language and be very conscious of my behavior when in his presence.

Dee-Bo required an enormous amount of patience and tolerance. His psychological wounds ran deep. He used vulgarity to cover his scars and threw out vitriol to defend his appearance.

"Shorty, it ain't a'ight to fuck with faggies," I approached this delicate subject with Dee-Bo on the second day. "You got a reputation for bein' freaked-out."

"I be hittin' Little Momma to pass the time," Dee-Bo endeavored to defend himself. "I ain't no faggy."

"If you're not a faggy," I countered, "You wouldn't be having sexual relations with a person who has the same genitalia as you."

"I ain't no muthufuckin' faggy," Dee-Bo came toward me in a threatening manner.

"Don't make me break your little puny ass up," I abandoned my avuncular demeanor. "I come back to the cell, and I see a homosexual leaving. What do you want me to call it?"

"All these other niggas 'round here be doin' it too," Dee-Bo was emphatic as he took a step back from me.

I recall telling Dee-Bo that his sexual preference was of no consequence to me. If he was into boys, that was his thing. I would respect him no less. However, gangsta etiquette demanded that I find another cell-buddy if he was into homosexuality.

Decorum and personal prejudices would not permit me to share a cell with someone who was openly gay. "Prison don't make you gay. It's designed to make you less than a man," I expressed with compassion. "But you gotta insist on being a man." Dee-Bo sat down on the chair and I sat on my bunk. It was time for me to communicate some truths to Dee-Bo that he might find unsettling; it was for the best that he got comfortable.

"This prison shit can't work unless we're made weak," I offered. "The men in the system gotta be killed off if they can't be broken. Prisons are built to profit off the backs of broken and defeated people."

I explained to Dee-Bo that it was no accident that prison officials make it quite difficult for us prisoners to maintain progressive relationships with women who show us a romantic interest, but make it exceedingly easy for us to engage in homosexuality. Dee-Bo and I shared scores of examples where corrections officers harassed prisoners' wives or girlfriends during visits, but did everything humanly possible to accommodate homosexual relationships. I had supposed that effeminate black males amuse the all-white guard staff in Hagerstown or at least do not present a threat to them.

I let Dee-Bo know that travelling through prison is a spiritual journey. It is a very personal and private affair and not a communal experience. If Dee-Bo was to be successful, that is, not become downtrodden, he must hold onto his morals and principles. He had to value good hygiene, masculinity and all the things he imagined to be virtuous and honorable.

Dee-Bo and I conversed for about three hours without interruption. Breakfast was called at four o'clock that morning. When I awoke at about 3:30 to brush my teeth and wash my face, Dee-Bo was still in his bunk, sleeping. I was shocked when I returned from breakfast and Little Momma ran out of my cell. It was an arduous task, but eventually, I convinced Dee-Bo that death is preferable to dishonor. In order to lead a noble and dignified life, you have to make your peace with death. Acquaint yourself with death and look for it everywhere you go. Imagine death in every form it takes. Invision your own death. Meditate upon your own end. Summon the courage to author your very own eschatology. Otherwise, you will be a coward. Life's greatest challenges will frighten you and possibly reduce you to a eunuch.

Prison is simply another great challenge in life. Poverty, brutality, hopelessness and loneliness launch one vicious attack after another against a prisoner.

Nothing about prison is fair. Might is always what is right in prison. Nepotism and cronyism are common practices. A prisoner who is weak and clingy will likely commit himself to thralldom while in prison.

The only way to successfully survive prison is to be prepared to abandon everything in an instant. Your most valuable possessions must be the ideals you hold in your heart. For a prisoner, that which is inside of him has to be greater than all that is behind or in front of him. If what a prisoner values most is not inside of him, he will surely be defeated. A prisoner does not hold dominion over his life; others do. A prisoner cannot maintain even the illusion of control. The modern prison system can only work if it is populated by men and women whose spirits have been broken.

Practicing a humility that is not the function of your conviction, but rather a response to intimidating circumstances makes you a coward. Engaging in homosexual activity because no women are available makes you weak. A man worthy of great esteem and reverence must be ready to have a greater impact on his environment than his environment can have on him.

In *The Soul of Black Folks*, W.E.B. Du Bois wrote:

There is in this world no such force as the force of a man determined to rise. The human soul cannot be permanently chained.

A prison's design is reliant upon chaining a man's spirit. It cages the body and institutes a variety of techniques to break him down. In order for a prisoner to get a good job assignment, one that will allow him to earn enough money to support himself, he must operate as a sycophant. A prisoner must abdicate any character trait that prison officials find threatening or not conducive to the furtherance of prison security. A man has to be completely maligned, spiritually eviscerated, and humbled by castigation before he can find contentment in prison.

It did not take long for me to realize that Roxbury's clean and pristine environment was not there to remind me of my own humanity. The wonderful smell of the grass and flowers and the picturesque mountains that surrounded the compound mocked my humanity. They showed me that I stood close to humanity, but I am not really human. Once I came to prison, it was my responsibility to maintain my humanity and all the dignities that it entails. You cannot depend on prison officials to restore all that is good inside of you.

Chapter XI

Loving, Teaching and Fighting

It did not take long for me to realize that everything I was, am and will be was under assault. Hagerstown officials felt uneasy in the presence of young, intelligent black men. If I were to go unmolested by the white officials at Roxbury, I would have to behave like a buffoon. I was far too in love with the man that I had become to turn back. I had acquired some traits that I was proud of. I possessed a moral compass and a personal constitution that could not be violated under any circumstances. I would never pretend to be less than who I am so that others would feel comfortable around me.

Still, I tried to make it work at Hagerstown even if I did not try very hard. I was respectful to the officials, but not in a manner that would suggest that I was obsequious. I used profanity in some of my verbal exchanges, but I was never vulgar. I was desperate to be a good example to Dee-Bo and the other young prisoners who were observing me. I had a formal education and a lot of street as well as penitentiary smarts. I was good-looking and my gravitas was undeniable. I inspired envy, love or pure hatred. No one could relate to me with indifference. A week had not lapsed before I was at loggerheads with the prison officials at Roxbury.

What made matters worse, my wife, Francine, was urging me to capitulate and make compromises to my dignity in order to go unmolested.

It was during our very first visit at Roxbury. Francine and I had not seen each other in more than a week. We came toward each other to embrace in the crowded visiting room. While she was in my arms, she looked directly into my eyes with anxiety and said, "The officer at the desk wasn't gonna let me in."

"What?" I was incredulous. Francine kissed me. I enjoyed the softness of her body and the taste of her tongue.

Afterward, she and I sat down opposite each other in the plastic chairs. We held hands and let our legs touch. We were still newly-weds, married less than a year.

"We're gonna have to contact headquarters so I can get special permission to visit you," Francine announced.

"Why?"

"Cause I'm an ex-convicted felon," Francine was matter-of fact. "They wasn't going to let me in today."

"How you get in?" I questioned.

"Just like you told me," she seemed proud. "I wouldn't accept no from someone who didn't have the authority to say yeah."

My wife was someone that I admired. The officer at the front desk informed her that because she was once convicted of a felony, she could not enter the institution without prior permission from the warden or headquarters. Francine had asked to see the warden or someone from headquarters. She had driven for well over an hour to make the visit to Hagerstown and was not going to be easily turned away.

A lieutenant was available to speak to her, but only the warden could permit her to visit me. Francine then insisted on speaking with the warden.

"Never accept no from a person who can't answer yes," my grandfather had taught me, and I taught that same lesson to Francine. Folks not high enough in the hierarchy of a bureaucratic institution are trained to systematically deny people certain things. Protocol does not give officers discretion; they must behave as automatons. If it is written in the book that anyone ever convicted a felony must not enter the institution to visit without prior approval from the warden, then that is exactly what the officers will adhere to. No one would consider the fact that Francine and I were permitted to marry and, therefore, she was allowed to visit me.

Once Francine registered to visit at the front desk, the computer showed that she had been convicted of theft some ten or fifteen years before.

"Pum," I called Francine by the pet-name I had given her, "I ain't gonna be here long. I'ma make these muthafuckas send me outta here."

"Ain't it betta here?" I found the question to be futile. "It looks clean and look at all this space in here." Yes, I could not deny that Roxbury was much cleaner and more spacious than the penitentiary. The visiting room was much more comfortable. There was no physical barrier to separate us like there was at the penitentiary. We touched and held hands during the entire visit. That could only happen at special times at the penitentiary in Baltimore.

I tried to explain why I could not stay in Hagerstown, "We're locked in all the time, baby. These white folks expect you to kiss ass and eat shit all day, every day."

Francine offered some rhapsody about me complying with the rules. "I can't adjust to this shit. If I adjust to this prison shit, I won't be any good to anybody out there in the free world."

In some respect, Francine became my false comforter like Job's wife from the Bible. Francine insisted that if I "played the game right," then I might be granted parole. "Pum, it doesn't matter how good or bad I am. Parole isn't a realistic option for me," I explained. "I was charged with multiple murders. I don't have a rape case or an accidental murder case. I was convicted of an 'I meant it' murder. If I were to be released from prison, it would have to be through the court via the judiciary process."

It was becoming tiresome trying to convince Francine that I needed money to mount a meaningful challenge to my imprisonment. I was not guilty of the crime for which I stood convicted, but I was far from innocent. Hell, I was never innocent. The Pollyanna notions Francine presented were becoming annoying, tedious, and aggravating. I was simply who I was. I felt no abiding need or desire to explain myself to anyone for any reason. However, Francine wasn't just some woman I was messin' around with. She was my wife. I had pledged a vow before God and my family and friends that I would cleave to this woman and become of one flesh with her. I did not reserve the right to lie to Francine or say anything to her that was hurtful. She was my partner.

Francine surrendered to my embrace as we stood to end the visit. She wore African fashioned clothing that allowed me to stick my arms into the folds of her dress so that I could actually feel her flesh if I dared - her entire womanly body.

"I'ma do my best to make it work, Pum-Pum."

Francine knew how to use her femininity to win me over. I had to chastise her a time or two about using her affection as a bargaining tool in our marriage. Her affection belonged to me; it was not something that I should ever have to compete for.

I started to feel like I was fighting too many battles. But actually, I was fighting only one huge war: the war for my soul. The prison officials, via an assortment of mechanisms, were trying to break my spirit and reduce me to docility. My wife was becoming just another instrument that prison officials seemingly used in their effort to make me passive.

Roxbury's daily routine conditioned inmates to be automatons. Breakfast in housing unit four was at four o'clock in the morning. Once we returned from the dining hall, we locked in until nine o'clock recreation. At 9:45 a.m. we were locked in our cells again for about thirty minutes. At 10:15, we· went to lunch. Once we exited the dining hall after the lunch meal, we locked in until one o'clock. If it was our yard or gym day, we went to either recreational area. But most days, three to four in a week, we were restricted to the recreational room located on the same tier we were assigned.

Roxbury was a very large institution, but we inmates were confined to a very small portion of the prison.

It was not lost on me that I had more room to operate and roam in the relatively small penitentiary than I had in that large prison in Hagerstown. All the Hagerstown cells were double, although the prison was built for single cell occupancy. The place was overcrowded and uncomfortable. I was finding it difficult to get the needed time to pray, meditate, think, read and grow spiritually.

Dee-Bo always seemed to find a reason to come to the cell whenever I was there. He enjoyed being around me and he had quickly become my annoying little brother. In some respects, I appreciated Dee-Bo's constant presence. When he was around, I operated from my highest level of understanding. I was conscious of my speech and courteous toward others. I never allowed my verbiage to descend into vulgarity.

I had persuaded Dee-Bo to read some classic works, like Dicken's *Tale of Two Cities* and Ralph Ellison's *Invisible Man.* In a brief period of time, I had convinced Dee-Bo that the power of the tongue was exponentially more powerful than a gun or a knife.

"If you arm yourself with a powerful voice," I told Dee-Bo, "You will never need a gun. Load your personal lexicon with beautiful words that resonate with souls, and the world will adore you and grant you your every wish."

I had grown exhausted by Dee-Bo's excessive cursing. Every other word from his mouth was a profanity. He started to grate on my hearing sense. Of course, when I confronted Dee-Bo about his swearing, he fought me, "You be cussin' too."

Yes, I often employed vulgarities to express my thoughts and sentiments. I was no Puritan by any stretch of the imagination. But I was making a paradigm shift. My wife had convinced me to stop selling illegal narcotics to supplement my meager state income. My friend, Lil Ronald, and a couple others had been helping me remain solvent as I journeyed through the prison system. I would be supplied with a narcotic connection, but I had to create my own agency to get the drugs and put the money into my account. Francine wasn't having any of it. She believed that she earned enough money to sustain me. " Pum-Pum," I oft pleaded with Francine as we faced one financial issue after another. "Holla at Ronald. Get what he got for me. I'll get it from you, and we'll have the money we need to fund my legal challenge and pay other bills."

I had always hustled. Prior to marrying Francine, I supported myself by selling narcotics in the prison. I had no mother, father or siblings to rely on for financial support. I had only myself. Once Francine came into my life, I had to start considering her feelings and interests. She suffered when I would get involved with violent confrontations over my dealings. It depressed her to see me on segregation. Drug dealing in prison creates a lot of drama. When Francine visited me during those days, she endured more intrusive searches and inspections.

"We decide things together," Francine was adamant. "I'm your wife. I'm not just some broad you're fuckin' with."

I was not accustomed to making compromises. My life was totally my own. I suffered the consequences of my decisions alone. I was an orphan. **Loneliness was my constant and most reliable companion.**

The vicissitudes of the drug trade and the hardships borne out from the decisions I had made influenced me to try doing things Francine's way. I had been in prison for well over a decade at that point. My off and on relationships with Joy, Annette and whatever girl who came in between them had grown tedious. I was enchanted by what Francine offered. I was presented with the opportunity to have a family. But I had to behave responsibly and maturely. I had to think more about living than dying. I had to abandon the ways of a Lothario.

It was difficult. From the beginning of life, I was taught a single game: Do or Die. We used to pretend that everything we earned was 'for keeps'. But as a drug-dealing, murdering hedonist navigating poverty, ignorance, and loneliness I had to quickly come to grips with the fact that everything comes to an end. The game of Do or Die's most emphatic rule is that you cannot hold onto anything for long, let alone forever. Long before I learned the scholarly word "eschatology" or philosophically studied death and endings, I knew about them. From a visceral perspective, I was made aware of such things.

The only way that anything, whether it be relationships, material objects or even life itself could be enjoyed is to know that it will end. Complete acceptance of that reality, that all things end allows the custodian of that knowledge to author his own endings.

Francine wanted to be married to me. She did not want to compete for my attention with anyone. I had grown exhausted by my former relationships. My girlfriend, Joy would be in my life for three to six months, then would vanish to pursue something more promising and less monotonous. Annette would come and stay less than that. The benefit of Joy and Annette, however, was that they both were pragmatic about my situation.

They had no qualms about meeting up with Lil Ronald or anyone I associated with who was willing to aid me in an illegal enterprise. They understood the importance of a hedonist having what he wanted when he wanted it. Besides, when I profited, they profited. Francine, on the other hand, wanted absolutely nothing to do with illegalities.

Francine was nine years my senior. She had spent some time in prison and had overcome a long struggle with drug addiction. Though she was leading a "square's life," she was no square. She was not naïve. Francine was intimately aware of the street life, illegal drug-dealing, and the manifold pitfalls that accompany such a life.

"You don't have a family, Tray. Your mother, father, Aunt Kim, and grandmother are dead. Everybody in your life is just fair-weather friends or whatever," she went on to let me know that she would not continue to be some bitch I was fuckin' with. She was offering me a genuine commitment.

I tried to explain to Francine that no prisoner can commit to anyone or anything forever. I was sentenced to life. I was subjected to a life where nothing was permanent. The only way that I could succeed was to make peace with death and with endings.

The only time that truly mattered was the moment, and if the moment I was in was to be the end, then I was okay with it. I was blessed not to have to suffer through the anxieties and frustrations that those who fear death do. I came to understand, quite early in life, that all things come to an end - so that new things can begin.

It is foolish then and contradicts the maxim that God personifies goodness and mercy to see death as evil. The one thing that we all have in common is death. All that exists will reach an end. Given that God is the Creator of all, it stands to reason that the end will be good and merciful, for that is what God is.

My understanding of life and appreciation of the man that I had become made it impossible for me to stay at Roxbury or any penal institution like it. I could not walk with my back bowed in a constant state of inferiority. I valued Francine and our marriage. I learned to appreciate some of the small benefits that being moved to a medium security prison provided. But I did not cling to anything. My entire biography spoke to the fact that I would let go in an instant.

It was time for lunch and I had entered the dining hall with Bobby Steward, Brown-Bey and Mo-Black. We all had come from the penitentiary and wanted to discuss our respective experiences at Roxbury.

Bobby Stewart had been at Roxbury the longest. Mo-Black and Brown-Bey came there two to three weeks before me. They were encouraging me to "just hang in there" and try to adjust to the new environment. I was being assured that Hagerstown was not that bad once you learned the routine, got a job assignment and got yourself used to the programs there.

The four of us were having a nice conversation. We had arranged ourselves in the chow line so that we could be together to eat our meal. The officials at Roxbury did not allow inmates to sit wherever they wanted. We had to fill in the seats as we picked up our food trays and came out of the two separate lines. If you desired to sit with someone specific, you had to maneuver yourselves into the lines as to come out together. It seems complicated, but it made sense after a while.

This young, muscular guy stepped in the line between Mo-Black and me. He was eager to sit with his friends too, I suppose.

"My man," Mo-Black tried to be diplomatic. "We have counted off."

"I ain't hearin' that shit," the young guy was rather belligerent.

I picked up a metal food tray and slapped the young guy across the face with it. I used all the force I could summon. I dropped the tray to the floor and before the guy could gather his wits, I hit him square in the jaw with my right fist. The blood spilling from his face and broken jaw were too much for him to comprehend. The angry young man collapsed at my feet just as six or seven officers rushed over and pushed me up against the concrete wall. I was restrained from inflicting more damage.

My hands were cuffed behind my back, and I was escorted from the dining hall by three officers. The pandemonium that had erupted in the dining hall settled down after that. The officer who maintained his grasp upon me as we walked down the compound toward housing unit four asked me, "What the hell was that all about?"

"I don't know," I deadpanned. "The muthafucka made me mad."

"That guy's an asshole," one of the other officers had said. "I knew somebody would eventually get him."

The officers seemed impressed by my pugilistic skills. I was shocked by the fact that I was being escorted to my regular cell as opposed to an isolation cell in the segregation unit.

"Take care of yourself," the officer said as he escorted me to my cell. "If you want me to testify at your adjustment, I'm Sgt. Martin."

My cell door was opened, I stepped inside, the handcuffs were removed from my wrist and the cell door was closed again. It was eerily quiet on the tier. The others had not returned from lunch. I laid down on my bunk and wanted to assess the situation. It had all happened so fast. I had gone out at about eleven o'clock for the meal. Mo-Black, Brown-Bey, Bobby Stewart and I embarked on the near half mile trek to the dining hall. For the past two and a half weeks, the four of us walked to meals and sat together without incident. We were simply four old-school dudes from the penitentiary trying to help each other adjust to the radical change of environment. It was seemingly unfathomable that someone would bother us. That young guy had to have been on some drugs. Either that or he just didn't realize who I was.

The others were returning from lunch now. Bobby Stewart was the first to come to the cell door.

"Tray," I heard his voice come through from the side of the cell door.

I remained on my back, my hands behind my head, serving as a pillow, "Yeah, Bobby. What's up?"

"Come to the door, you stupid muthafucka!" There was the feared condemnation.

"I know what you gonna say, Bobby," I was matter-of-fact as I came to the door.

"You don't know shit," Bobby offered in a good-natured manner. "Look, you ain't have a ticket in a while, so you'll probably only get thirty to forty-five days on lock-up."

"Cool," I was not concerned about trivial matters. "When will they pack me up and take me over?"

"You gotta get outta that penitentiary shit, man," Bobby answered. "Up here you go up for the ticket first. If you get found guilty, then you go over to lock-up."

"So you think I can beat the ticket?" It was a rhetorical question.

"You ain't that stupid, is you?" I wondered whether that was a rhetorical question as well.

Bobby's consummate sense of humor was on full display. "Don't nobody beat tickets up here. Just lay back and enjoy your

TV and music for a couple days and get yourself a few books together to take over and that be that."

I noticed the lights on the tier flick off and on to signal that the cell doors were about to come open. Every inmate had to go stand by his cell door to lock in. All the doors on the tier opened except mine. Dee-Bo stood outside too. Once all the other cell doors were closed, my cell door opened and Dee-Bo stepped in. He was excited to see me. "Unc, you got it in," the grin on Dee-Bo's face was infectious. "You knocked that nigga out and broke his shit."

I did not feel any pride about what had transpired in the dining hall. This was not the example I wanted to set.

"I wish that didn't happen, young," I told Dee-Bo. I couldn't think of anything else to say. I had not developed enough to apologize for attacking someone who I felt had slighted me. The young guy I had beat up was a bully. His rudeness demonstrated that much. His rudeness also strongly suggested to me that he was a weak person, for rudeness is a weak man's imitation of strength. Men of strength and nobility are generally polite, courteous and respectful of others.

"Dontae ain't gonna want no get back," Dee-Bo had said to me as I sat down in the chair. "Nigga go for bad up here, but he don't wanna go at you penitentiary niggas."

"I ain't concerned about Dontae wantin' revenge," I communicated to Dee-Bo. "I hope this doesn't end in more pointless violence over this small, meaningless shit."

"Unc, you gettin' ready to start preachin' that pro-black, don't-kill-another-brotha shit?"

I had to laugh. "Naw, I ain't gonna do that. You already know."

In the short time that Dee-Bo and I had shared the cell, I was able to impress upon him that wisdom had no place for violence. Fools and idiots resorted to violence. Smart people used their minds to intelligently get done what they needed.

"Dee-Bo, I broke that man's shit because I wanted to sit at a particular table in the dining hall," I confessed. "Now I gotta listen to my wife's lecture, deal with her tears and do this lock-up shit."

"Fuck that nigga," Dee-Bo was emphatic.

"Didn't you say young's name was Dontae?" I asked.

It was important for me to reference Dontae by his name. I did not want to divorce him from his humanity by calling him a nigga or muthafucka. I had come to realize that it was only possible for me to inflict violence upon another person if I first dehumanized him. I don't quite know when that realization had come to me. But there it was - in my conscience. The quiet times I had spent in segregation units, alone with my private thoughts and agonizing over life's mysteries, had acquainted me with the accumulated wisdom of the ages. While I could not run away from my violent past, I could never again be comfortable there.

I had a formal education. I was married to a loving, albeit annoying, woman who genuinely cared about me. Drew Leder, Father Tim Brown and other professors at Loyola had devoted time and energy to help me develop a moral compass rooted in philosophical principles. I was fully human, and if I deigned to deny someone else his or her humanity, I would lose elements of my own.

Of course, that high-flying moral shit was diametrically opposed to the creed I had lived. In the ghetto streets, on the penitentiary tiers and through the struggles of poverty and degradation, only the strong will survive. Right and wrong were predicated by what served your interests and desires - not by some sense of moral, philosophical notions. Long ago, I had been told this Zulu Proverb: The child with the full belly said to the child with the empty belly, "Be of good cheer."

My creed had said it was up to me to be the child with the full belly, and if my belly was empty and I was told to be of good cheer, I was to ignore such guidance and kill the muthafucka who suggested it. Do or die is the primary game of life. We are all charged with playing it. The challenge that everyone faces is suffering. Suffering is the cost we must pay to live.

"Call my wife, Dee-Bo," I instructed as I wrote the number on a piece of paper. "Her name is Francine. Tell her I'm on lock-up or whatever this shit is. Explain to her how this shit goes. Tell her I ain't stayin' in this muthafuckin' jail. Let her know I'll write her, but don't expect no phone calls from me. Tell her not to come up here to visit."

The truth is, in Hagerstown, the entire atmosphere seemed to serve as my antithesis and threaten my very existence. Every philosophical notion I subscribed to was out of place at Roxbury. Moreover, a significant portion of the inmate population there ostracized me. They wanted me to cling to the nothing that the officials at Roxbury offered and be content and complacent.

I was serving a life sentence and, therefore, was not eligible to participate in most of the programs there. The vocational training classes that taught marketable trade skills were for inmates with one to three years remaining and with a mandatory release date.

Functions where I might have sexual contact with my wife were an alien concept in Hagerstown. The only inmates housed in single cells were the ones who had a history of mental illness. Everyone else was double-celled. I would be afforded absolutely no privacy during which I could pray, cry and grow. My friends and family could not possibly afford the enormous cost of the long-distance telephone calls. And, the hour and a half travel time to visit was hardly worth it if you factored in the racist shit your family and friends would face when they came to the Hagerstown region.

Life's challenges did not frighten me, nor did they make a coward out of me. I had no qualms about ending things — and there rests my genius. I refused to accept that there were times when one simply had no choice in a given situation. Humans always have a choice. Of all the animals God created, man alone does not have to submit to his natural instincts. If a dog is in heat, it has to mate. A horny human does not. When a lion is hungry, it has to feed on whatever is available. A human can fast for any number of reasons. If an animal feels physically threatened, it has to strike. We, humans, can choose passivity. Hell, humans are the only animal that can kill ourselves if we find our choices unpleasant, and therein lies our source of panic and anxiety.

"Ms. Francine is mad," Dee-Boo announced as he entered the cell. "She started cryin' and askin' me questions about everything."

I should not have asked a boy to convey such a delicate and serious message to a fragile and fickle-minded woman. I had to learn how to better manage sharing my life with another.

"You let her know that I was okay?" I asked.

"She knows you ain't dead," he answered. "I told her 'bout the fight and you said don't come up on a visit 'cause she might not get in."

Dee-Bo communicated my message to Francine as best he could and I was grateful. I was satisfied that she would not be wasting her time and money to drive from Baltimore to Hagerstown for naught.

I made up my mind that I was going to force the officials at Roxbury to transfer me to Jessup. I was not going to wait at least a year to be eligible for transfer.

The day after Dee-Bo had called Francine on my behalf, the opportunity presented itself for me to force that transfer. The 4-12 p.m. guards had come on duty. The officers were conducting their routine "bar-check."

My cell door was opened, and Dee-Bo and I were seated on our bunks. A corrections officer came into the cell to check the windows and bars as protocol required. However, this particular officer decided to reach under the bunk, pull out my tennis shoes and started kicking them around the cell.

I was calm as I said "Those are $150 Jordan's. Please stop mishandlin' my shit."

"Fuck your sneakers," was his retort. "You monkeys come up here from the pen."

I heard nothing else. I flew into an absolute rage. I hit the offending corrections officer in the face and he fell into the locker. I heard a television hit the floor and shatter. I felt a punch or two land on my face and into the back of my head, but I felt no pain. I bit fingers, kicked faces and tried to maul out the eyes of every officer I could reach. I used every electric appliance in the cell as a weapon. I endeavored to inflict as much damage as I possibly could. I was determined to not get pinned down.

Dee-Bo had lept from the top bunk and ran from the cell as soon as I threw the first punch. Two other officers rushed into the cell and started hitting me. I felt their punches, but I maintained my focus and rage on the officer before me, who had started the shit.

More officers came into the cell and I was pepper-sprayed. I was beaten into submission and soon enough I was unconscious. When I returned to consciousness, I was on a stretcher on my way to the infirmary for medical treatment. My eyes were too swollen to focus on anything. My lips were busted and swollen and my body ached. I had been severely beaten, but I was far from a defeated man.

Chapter XII

Unleashed to Self-destruct

I agonized in pain for about two weeks. My ribs were cracked and the cut over my eye required four stitches. I found it difficult to breathe or even move. I laid in bed for about a month. I was not permitted access to my mail and was prohibited from using the telephone. I was completely isolated. Only medical and correctional personnel could speak to me.

There was no doubt in my mind that Francine was sitting at home in a panic. She was likely calling nonstop in hopes of gaining access to me. She and I used to talk almost every day. More than two weeks had passed and we had not spoken once. Word had likely gotten out that I had been jumped by the guards at Roxbury. I had no clue about what was going on with Francine or any of my other loved ones. My primary focus was on getting well. I felt powerless and ashamed as I laid in bed like some kind of invalid.

"We got ourselves a mess here, Mr. Jones," Lt. Barnhart said as he sat in a chair next me. "Sergeant Yost told me everything."

I did not feel like talking because such a task was a struggle for me. I just closed my eyes and listened. Lt. Barnhart told me that his investigation had discovered that Officer Shoemaker had, in fact, said things to me that were incendiary and bigoted. But I didn't need anybody to tell me what I already knew.

"Once you get discharged from here," Lt. Barnhart had said, "We're gonna send you down to Jessup. You'll probably do better there."

That settled everything for me. The Cut, the Maryland House of Corrections in Jessup was a relic built in either the late nineteenth century or early twentieth century. The Cut was not as old as the penitentiary, but it was far from modern like Roxbury. In fact, the structure of the Cut was very similar to that of the penitentiary. The Cut had four tiers of cells stacked on top of one another and the penitentiary had five. There were multiple dormitories in the Cut whereas the penitentiary had only one.

The Cut was rampant with violence and systematic corruption. I would feel right at home there.

Lt. Barnhart informed me that I had to settle the infraction notice that I had received for the fight in the dining hall. I would go before an adjustment hearing officer for that. No reports or notice of infraction would be made about the encounter I had with Officer Shoemaker. Once I had healed enough, I would be taken to Housing Unit Five, the segregation unit, to serve out however much disciplinary segregation time I was given.

It took sixty-two days for me to heal. On the day that I was discharged from the infirmary, the institution's adjustment hearing representative came to me and said, "Jones, plead guilty and you'll get forty-five days on lock-up."

I accepted the offer. It had been at least four years since my last stint in segregation. The forty-eight hours that I had spent in isolation for refusing to submit to the humiliating strip-search upon entering Roxbury did not register at the time. While I did not look forward to the loneliness and other such tortures I would surely experience in segregation, I did look forward to ending my time at Roxbury. Hell, I loved endings. I wanted to get back into an environment where I would be more comfortable. The serenity and regimented routine in Hagerstown were unsettling for me.

The overwhelming relief I felt on that cold December day in 1996 when I was transferred to the Cut cannot be described using words. I was transported to Jessup in a blue prison van. I was the only one, which made it obvious that my transfer was a matter of special circumstances.

I was silent throughout the hour and a half drive to Jessup. I suppressed my gregarious nature and assumed a regal poise. The corrections officers charged with transporting me oozed hostility. I understood human nature enough to know that politeness in response to hostility is like heat to a candle; it would melt it away. I was not troubled by the hostility the officers felt toward me. Their sentiments caused them discomfort and that knowledge alone delighted me. My countenance at the time only added to their grief.

It required an enormous effort on my part to pretend that I did not desire to converse with the officers during that long drive. I had just spent forty-five days in isolation and a friendly conversation accompanied by some good music would have made that journey a decent experience at least. Perhaps I would have asked the officers why they hated me. They may have provided me with some kind of explanation.

Alas, I must voyage through life knowing that I hated those officers simply because they hated me. And that, of course, is a stupid reason to hate. For hatred is the source of self-destruction. If I am to harbor hatred in my heart and mind, for even an instant, I want there to be a good reason for it. A physiological and spiritual price is paid for hating. That knowledge rests within my conscience. I cannot reference a source other than intuition to confirm the truth of that.

While indifference is the essence of man's inhumanity, to man hatred is the primary source for his self-destruction. Whenever I hate, I want a damn good reason for doing so. It is a dangerous emotion and must be secured in a safe place outside the human soul and heart. I suggest under some tree or close enough, but in a distance place.

I entered the Cut unwittingly posed to self-destruct. I was in full hedonist mode and gave no consideration to the fact that since time immemorial, man has not been able to separate pleasure from pain. It was late morning or early noon when I arrived at the Cut. Once the Hagerstown officers unshackled me, I was told by an officer at Jessup, "Take your property and find your way to E-3. It's on the west-wing."

I was not strip-searched. My personal property was not inventoried. I was simply unleashed and charged with finding my own way through the jungle. The very first familiar face I saw once I stepped out into the corridor was that of a dear friend, Derick Davis.

“My muthafuckin’ nigga, Bo-Jingles,” I warmly greeted Derick with my arms wide open and a smile as bright as the sun.

“There you go wid that Bo-Jingles shit, nigga,” Derick warmly accepted my embrace and handshake. ”We knew yesterday you was comin’ down here. You on the tier with me, Tatar, World and Marty.”

Derick was a rather handsome man. He had smooth brown skin and evenly shaped teeth that offered a brilliant smile. Derick was relatively short and comically bow-legged. Hence the sobriquet, Bo-Jingles. No one aside from Derick’s closest friends and relatives could call him Bo-Jingles. Two people were brutally stabbed at the penitentiary for addressing Derick as Bo-Jingles.

“Where’s at, nigga?” I had abandoned all the progressive, life-affirming knowledge that I had painstakingly attained in that instant.

“Your man, KC, is a’ight,” Derick let me know who had some narcotics.

Derick went off to find a cart to help me carry my three boxes to the cell I was assigned. Within an hour of arriving at the Cut, I was in the courtyard reacquainting myself with the friends and associates I had made at the penitentiary. There was also an assortment of folks in the Cut that I had known from uptown in free society.

I was looking for Kenny Caldwell, KC. Derick had informed me that he was hustling and distributing heroin. My rapport with KC was undeniably strong. The moment he realized that I had arrived at the prison, etiquette dictated that he provided me with a gratuity.

KC was in the courtyard, sitting in the bleachers among three or four acquaintances I recognized from various places. "What's poppin', KC?" I greeted my friend. We shook hands, embraced and then I greeted the others.

"How in the hell you end up in Hagerstown?" KC inquired.

"They ain't realize I was a false-alarm," I answered. "I ain't catch no tickets or fuck nobody up in a minute; they thought I went soft."

In my last three years at the penitentiary, I devoted myself to my studies. I wanted to successfully matriculate the college program and secure my Bachelor's Degree. I did that; I also fell in love with philosophy. I pursued knowledge and ultimately examined my own life. I was persuaded, after studying the teachings of Socrates, **that an unexamined life isn't worth living.** During that period of my life, I had become reacquainted with Francine, strengthened my relationship with her and married her.

"Yo, I can help you get on your feet when you get ready," KC told me as we stood up and walked away from the others. "My people hollin' at me heavy."

I was not ready to take on any narcotics to sell. I wanted a small amount for personal use. The dormant addict in me materialized, "What you holdin'?"

"I ain't got nothing but a little bit of dope right now."

"Cool," I answered too quick and grinned with too much enthusiasm. The hedonistic angle of my personality was demanding expression.

KC gave me enough heroin to share with Derick. I wanted some marijuana, my preferred drug, but none was immediately available. I had to find another source for that.

I put my mendicant's bowl out, and before an hour had lapsed, I had marijuana to smoke and cocaine to go along with my heroin. I locked into my assigned cell for the 3:30 p.m. count to commence self-destructing. Prior to coming to the Cut, I had stopped praying and studying. I did not bother to take the one day out of every week to fast and focus my attention to what the universe had to reveal to me.

When the officials at Roxbury put me in segregation for forty-five days prior to my transfer, I used the time to read novels that glorified violence, criminality and vengeance. In short, I dropped my school-books and lost my lessons.

Wise counselors, teachers and other such guides had instructed me to be on guard for impulsive ideas that would result in all too familiar, stupid actions. It was communicated to me that if I pursued pleasure without consideration of all the inevitable pain that can come with it, I would hurt myself and those around me. Since the beginning of time, man has tried and failed to separate pleasure from pain. Pleasure and pain accompany each other devoutly.

Those of us born into poverty without parents to guide and love us tend to learn behaviors that perpetuate poverty, crime and imprisonment. Compound that with circumstances that I desired to escape; it required a concerted effort. I had to maintain a conscious understanding of everything I knew to be true and conduct all my affairs in accordance with that understanding. That was not easy to achieve, but well worth the endeavor.

Philosopher John Locke declared that the best defense in this world is a thorough knowledge of it. Things in this world will either serve to our benefit or detriment. Nothing is neutral. That is especially true of the soul. You must nurture the calls it makes within the silent regions of your mind. We all reach a point where we, as individuals, are in charge of what direction we will move in. The path you choose will decide your fate.

Providence has revealed to me that the man that harbors resentment in his heart will always choose a path that leads to self-destruction. Hatred is that sole emotion that operates in a very subtle manner. Hatred gives the impression that it wants to destroy or harm some external matter - and that may be true, but hate hesitates to reveal that it destroys all. It is especially destructive to the vessel that tries to contain it.

I failed to watch my thoughts through meditation. When I was placed into segregation after my release from the infirmary, rather than use the time to examine my thoughts and assess my life, I read those meaningless novels and idly passed time by talking out of the door to others. I was anxious to get into an environment that was violent and chaotic because chaos was familiar. The least tractable of the inmate population at the penitentiary was sent to the Cut, which is where I should have gone from the start.

Prison officials mistook my pursuit of a higher education to be something that it was not. While a formal education can contain the spirit and transform antisocial behavior, it had awoken a restlessness in me.

I was better than my circumstances. Nothing about the way things were pleased me. I was in a marriage that stifled me, and correctional officials had control over my life. God, the universe, or some external force had dealt me an awful hand. I was all that I had and, therefore, I would have to be all that I need. The state had condemned me to prison for life. I was told that I would never be allowed to return to free society because I was a cold-blooded murderer.

Everything that was said about me was untrue, but I did not have the resources or the necessary sophistication to defend myself against the accusations. I was like Mary Shelley's Frankenstein character; I took my clues on how to behave from my environment. I maintained the proper countenance, but I sometimes neglected my internal self-inventory and ongoing personal search. If I did not create silent moments, times of calm quietude, to look at the emotions and thoughts that were subtly guiding my decisions, a negative emotion like hate would have deleterious effects on me.

Fate called upon me to navigate some exceedingly challenging circumstances. I cannot have success on my journey without first building a character rooted in fortitude. I have to constantly see things and people for whatever they are and approach them with my highest understanding. I have to defend myself against anything that would render me inauthentic.

I am naturally loving and giving. I enjoy laughter and pleasant atmospheres. Chaotic and violent environments force me into a nonchalant attitude. I pretend to exude machismo to excite fear in others. I could never ignore the fact that all human acts are motivated by either fear or love. Experience, the greatest of all teachers, has shown me time and time again that I could get more done if people feared me rather than loved me. Surely, I wanted people to love me. Who doesn't? But in this material world I needed material things. Therefore, I needed to get things done. For only a ghost can live without materials.

I tacitly surrendered to hate. I was not going to rely on my wife or anyone else for financial support. I wanted to stand alone and consider no one else's needs in any of my decisions. I was an unapologetic hedonist. Pleasure was my chief goal. But my soul was not barren and bereft. I was loved, cared for and familiar enough with God. At no time in my life should I have been a 'bete noire.' I was simply reared in an environment riddled with crime and chaos. Hatred and fears of inferiority prevailed in the community that had raised me and the time I spent in the penitentiary fostered those sentiments.

Francine and I started having frequent arguments. She did not like me associating with Ronald or any of the others that were involved in illegal activities. I had formed a friendship with a fairly attractive young woman named Tracey and Francine had insisted that I end it.

I pointed out to Francine that all of her friends were men. Moreover, she had had romantic or sexual encounters with each of them. Tracey and I were in a purely platonic relationship. I was not going to end my friendship with a wonderful person to appease my wife's insecurity.

When Francine and I started seeing each other, she presented herself as my ideal partner. We knew each other before I went to prison. We were products of the same subculture. Francine was not supposed to have been some naïve prude. She had been around the block. I could not tolerate her new inhibitions. Matters of jealousy and possessiveness should not have entered into our relationship. She had convinced me that we would be guided by practicality.

"Baby, you can see who you wanna," I reasoned with Francine. "And I can't see nobody unless you approve."

"I'm your wife," Francine said. "I don't want no woman comin' here visitin' you other than your family."

Francine had a very close friendship with her ex-husband and two or three former boyfriends. I had been convinced that nothing could come between Francine and me, other than she and I. Trust was to be the hallmark of our relationship. I accepted that I would experience instances of inadequacy in our marriage. Francine was a reasonably attractive, gainfully-employed, intelligent woman. Any man would have been happy to have her. I was serving a life sentence in prison and that meant that I was hardly in a position to compete for her affection. She brought exponentially more to the marriage table than I did.

"Our marriage can't last unless I'm home with you, Pum," I finally told her. "For a marriage to last, three essential elements must be satisfied. There must be sexual fulfillment, financial support and emotional growth."

If any one of those elements is neglected, there will be infidelity. I could not fulfill Francine sexually or support her financially. I had a mature understanding of the situation at least. A woman could come to me and share her deepest secrets and feel no shame. I knew, as any bona fide male chauvinist would, that most women have an innate need to have a man in their life who they could share their innermost fears, desires and secrets with. Women want to feel like they are being wisely guided through life's obstacles.

The crucibles of life had forged my development. My radiance shined brightest in the darkest places. Francine was in an exceedingly low psychological place when our romance began. She was struggling with her bipolar disorder when I came into the dark with her and guided her into the light by sharing my enlightenment.

Francine promised to make me the number one priority in her life. If I live to be a thousand years old and well into my dotage, I will always be able to recall Francine's marriage proposal. "Tray, I'm tired of just bein' some woman you're messing' with. I wanna be your wife," she had said.

Francine had come to visit me earlier in the day, but I had been visiting with a former girlfriend, Joy. Francine was denied access to me. She was jealous and angry and, therefore, insisted upon marriage. I had to make her the main priority in my life if I was to be a priority in hers.

Francine pointed to the many things that rendered me desperate. "You ain't got no mother or father. Your grandmother is dyin' and your Aunt Kim is already dead," Francine compelled me to abandon any notion I had of myself and assume the inferior status of an impoverished prisoner in need of alms.

I loved my wife, but I resented her as well. Francine seemingly desired to eviscerate me. There was no such thing as compromising in our relationship. My wife had the upper-hand on me and she boldly asserted it. There wasn't any more sex at the functions. Francine decided to be active in trying to secure various rights for prisoners.

"Francine, bein' an activist for prisoners will drain you and take away from us," I warned.

"How?" she had asked. "You're selfish; you want everything to be about you."

"You damn right," I admitted. "If I don't overturn this conviction and get home to you, we ain't gonna work."

Francine insisted that she knew what was best for us, but she did not. Her activism took off; she was invited to civic and political events to speak about prison conditions, parole for men sentenced to life in Maryland and other wrongs or injustices that affect incarcerated men. Francine was visiting prisons throughout the state of Maryland as a prison volunteer. She developed such a wholesome, pristine good-girl reputation that she would not degrade herself by having sex with me at the functions in an open area.

There was no way that I would accept not getting some pussy every so often. I admired the Spartans, but I did not want to mimic them. "Pum-Pum, baby," I was being as kind as I could. "Whores go with pimps just like barbers go with manicurists. And square-ass-bitches should go with square-ass-niggas."

Francine and I were at a very difficult point in our relationship. We were thinking things that neither of us would give voice to. The very notion of divorce was anathema to us both. Our respective family and friends had advised us against marrying. We knew that nothing caused suffering and misery more than loving someone you had to be separated from or loving someone who is unlovable.

We had gotten ourselves into a marriage where the likelihood of success was remote. I would imagine there were moments when I was unlovable, and I know that Francine was not exactly lovable at times. The acrimony and recrimination that was present in our marriage made it impossible for either of us to be fully lovable.

"Francine, just do you. I don't give a fuck," I was exasperated. "I just don't wanna argue no more. I don't wanna fight."

We were at a function and Francine had refused to be intimate with me. I had to replace her; my journey was far too arduous to have to contend with my own wife.

I was desperate to secure judicial relief. Francine knew, maybe even more than I did, that **nothing is more motivated by economics than our criminal justice system.** Yet, she consistently refused to help me raise the necessary money to fund my legal endeavors.

I started selling dope. The lifestyle that had caused me ineffable grief and loss beckoned my return. There was no alternative way for me to earn the money I needed, and I had no family to rely on. My friend, Lil Ronald, was my life-line. His goal was to help me get free and not have to sacrifice clothing packages, commissary and other prison comforts in the pursuit.

"What up, homey?" I greeted Lil Ronald once he had answered his phone.

"Everything proper," he answered. "I'm just coolin'."

"Can I get twenty-eight of those?"

"You unleashed, huh?" I smiled and enjoyed a great laugh.

It had been four years since I last asked for an entire ounce of heroin. I had abandoned the business. The treachery of the illegal drug trade had grated against my newly developed sense of self. But I was ready to cut off my head before I lost any more hair.

Chapter XIII

Backward to Freedom

All the lessons I had learned seemed to have been forgotten the instant I entered The Cut. I understood most, if not all, the perils associated with narcotics. But there I was using and selling as if I had not experienced betrayal and lost at the hands of drugs in my lifetime. I would not allow myself to be counseled by anyone, except my Momma Boo, who did not encourage my involvement in such negativity.

Francine and I started to grow apart. She was active in prison reform efforts, which included attending various civic events, sponsoring some of them, speaking at churches and organizing the families of inmates serving life or other lengthy sentences to push through legislation that would favor us. I was becoming an embarrassment to her.

"Tray, you get caught up in this mess, how do I explain to folks that you deserve another opportunity to be free?" she hurled at me on more than one occasion.

My typical response was, "I don't give a fuck what you tell 'em. I'ma do me."

I had learned to ignore Francine's tears. She often used them to manipulate me and try to transform me into someone I was not. My situation was abnormal. The state had claimed that I was a hit-man for a notorious drug dealer operating out of East Baltimore. If I was not guilty of the murder for which I was convicted, it was assumed that I was guilty of some other murder. I was trapped in a desperate situation. It was abundantly clear to me that if I were to return to free society, the court would have to grant me relief. Court was not an option for people who had no money. The initiated accept that nothing is more motivated by economics than our judicial system.

I failed to explain to Francine that the law's primary focus is to regulate the affairs of those who have nothing. I was an inherent burden to anyone who dared to invite me into her life. My personal constitution would not permit me to rely on my wife, a woman I truly loved and respected, for financial support. My natural inclination was to be chivalrous. A man reliant upon a woman for financial support is everything that I found to be beneath masculine dignity. I wanted Francine to aid me as a partner. She could have facilitated matters between my friends and I.

She could have simply moved the funds as I directed. But she would not do anything that would result in me having financial independence.

The blissfulness of ignorance was no longer of any comfort to me. I was educated, and I knew that what I was doing was categorically wrong. In fact, I used drugs, marijuana and heroin to assuage my cognitive dissonance. I erected a moral constitution that allowed me to measure wrong from right by what suited my interest. In short, if it advanced my interest, it was right. If it did not, it was wrong.

It was far too frustrating to explain my philosophy. Unless a person actually walked in my shoes, he or she could not possibly understand my rationale. When I was merely a sixteen years old child, I was told that I was so fucked up that I would never be allowed back into free society. Prison was to be my home forever. It would not matter if I adjusted my character, became an upright Christian eligible for sainthood or an honorable and loyal husband, I was to be forever confined to prison.

How could my wife not appreciate what was before me? I had been incarcerated for well over a decade with no relief in sight. I was suffering the greatest of all human tragedies.

It is incalculable suffering to put a man in prison, confine him to such a small space and leave him there for his entire life. I would have been cast down among the foolish if I did not muster everything within my skill-set to overcome my predicament.

My life's circumstances were not a reflection of my innate qualities. I was so situated because of my opportunities, or lack thereof.

It had already been communicated to me that the world itself was made up of stolen goods. Those who have stolen the most establish the rules for the rest of us. Jesus, Himself, instructed us to give to God what is God's and to give to Caesar what is Caesar's. Immorality and corruption surrounded me. In that environment, I had to determine what belonged to God and what belonged to Caesar. To live in the world that I knew entailed danger and risks. I could not play host or pay homage to fear and realistically expect to be successful at any endeavor. It had always been a matter of life and death for me. In fact, in order for me live, I could not fear death. Hell, there were instances when I looked to death with enthusiasm.

Prison does not allow anyone to live. It simply permits one to breathe one's way through existence. Living involves maintaining some semblance of control over yourself, experiencing new challenges and being free from monotony. A man living life naturally supports his family and friends and is not a burden to anyone. He is relevant and meaningful to others and when his life is finished, those left behind will know that he once lived.

I needed $15,000 to hire Fred Bennett to represent me. He and I had consulted; Mr. Bennett had reviewed my entire trial transcript and other relevant documents related to my case. He felt reasonably sure that he could win a new trial for me. There were a number of irregularities that happened before, during and after my trial. In Mr. Bennett's written assessment of my case, he stated that, **"It is clear Mr. Jones was denied a fair trial..."**

Fred Bennett was among the best appellate attorneys in the state of Maryland during the 1990s. He had a great reputation for overturning criminal convictions and getting criminal defendants favorable results. But he was not cheap. My goal was to secure Mr. Bennett's legal service. I made that abundantly clear to Francine.

"Pum, I'm getting Fred Bennett," I informed Francine during a visit.

We were both convinced that our marriage would not survive much longer if I stayed in prison, separated from each other.

"I don't have Fred Bennett money," she said. "Why do you think I'm out here fighin' for parole for lifers?"

"I don't know why you do what you do," I was exasperated. "Under the best political circumstances, I'm not a candidate for parole."

Francine and I had had this conversation too many times, and I was not going to have it again. The allegation against me was that I had likely killed several people in furtherance of a criminal enterprise. If I were to get any relief, I had to access the court and win it through the judicial process.

I could appreciate that compromise is essential to a successful marriage. That was not beyond my comprehension. Moreover, I genuinely loved my wife and wanted our union to work. Therefore, I modified my tone and said as gently as I could, "I'm gonna need for you to set up a separate savings account for me. When money come to you for me, it's for Bennett."

"Where the money gonna come from?" Francine assumed naïveté.

"Various people. Sometimes it might be straight cash from somebody and other times somebody might send you a money order or a check from here. I'm doin' me," I was not being circumspect.

"No, I ain't doin' it."

I took a deep breath, then I crossed the Rubicon, "What good is you to me?" It was a rhetorical question. "You won't fuck at functions and you won't help me get the money I need to get outta here. I don't need this shit." I got up from my seat, left Francine sitting there and exited the visiting area without looking back. It would have been okay with me if our marriage had ended right then and there. My priority was to get free from prison. Winning Francine over was second or third on my list of things to do.

It was of no consequence to me how Francine would react to me leaving as I had. I was independent. I did not have to take into account anyone's feelings. My life was mine alone. Absent the one constant in my life, my Momma Boo, I would have collapsed under the weight of it all. No one could ever quite understand me and say the wisest things at the right moment as she did.

My Momma Boo had a way of making me feel special and comfortable with things as they presented themselves. Her love allowed me to feel a contentment and sense of security that no orphan typically feels.

While Momma Boo had three children of her very own, never once did she ever make me feel like I was second to any of them. In fact, Kirk, Momma Boo's oldest son, often joked that his mother liked me more than she did him. Of course, it was no joke. Momma Boo did like me more than she liked Kirk. She would never admit it, but it was obvious.

Momma Boo loved me as if I were one of her own children. One of my earliest memories of this love was from when I was about five or six years old. Kirk and I were playing a game called Skillet. He and I had started to fight and we were clumsily rolling around on the ground when Momma Boo came upon us. She separated us and refused to let us explain who started it. I somehow ended up in the back seat of Momma Boo's car with Kirk and his big sister, Yolanda. Their father, Joe, was at the wheel. We drove around to my house, just around the corner and Momma Boo informed my Aunt Kim, who was my legal guardian, that she was taking me to an ethnic festival that was taking place at the Inner Harbor. It was to be the first time that I sat close to Yolanda. I had a childhood crush on her. I sat between them in silence. I could not think of a single word to say because I was intimidated by Yolanda's presence, but was comforted by Momma Boo's.

Momma Boo had always been a calming constant in my life. She listened to me, offered no judgments and loved me through whatever mess I got myself into.

Francine would often, foolishly go to Momma Boo to try to convince her that I was doing one thing or another wrong, but Momma Boo always stood by me. She would not stand against me. She would listen to Francine and if her view aligned with Francine's, she would tell me in private. Momma Boo let me know that I had her absolute love and devotion and that has been the essence of my strength.

Everyone has to have that someone who puts him first no matter what. Usually it is that mother's love that guides you through hardship. I lacked that in my life and Momma Boo recognized that. She provided me with it. Whenever I called Momma Boo, she answered and never made me feel like I was a nuisance to her. It was painfully amusing at times, when Francine would try to enlist Momma Boo to dissuade me from my way of thinking.

Momma Boo understood that I was naturally stubborn. By simply loving me through my hurt, I will find the path that leads to happiness and prosperity. In my heart, I knew that I was verging. All the hurt and loss I had suffered were a result of my participation in illegal drug activity, the very thing that I was involved in once again. I had to stop, but I did not want

Francine to influence my decision. She had already exercised too great of an influence over me as if I were spineless.

Alas, I suppose that desperation prevents us all from thinking and behaving rationally. Humans need meditation, prayer and contemplation to become rational.

Time often serves as an elixir. The state tired of the rampant corruption at The Cut. A raid was executed on the Maryland House of Correction by state and federal officials. The prison was put on lock down for nearly a month as a thorough search for contraband went underway. Anyone suspected of any significant wrongdoing was gathered up and placed on Administrative Segregation to await transfer to distant prisons. Some were sent to prisons outside the state of Maryland. Several corrections officers were terminated. The Cut was reformed.

I was placed on Administrative Segregation. Prison officials contemplated transferring me out of state, but opted, instead, to transfer me to Eastern Correctional Institution (E.C.I.) in Westover, Maryland, which was far worse than Roxbury. The officials at E.C.I. were adamant about creating an inmate population that was absolutely docile. Inmates at that correctional facility were required to lock themselves in the cell whenever they returned from eating or recreating.

The cell doors at E.C.I. opened electronically, but they did not close. Inmates were called upon to pull the cell door close to lock themselves in. I found that practice to be humiliating.

I refused to do it. The officials there insisted that I should lock my cell door or I would be restricted to the cell. I would not be allowed any recreational privileges. I did not concern myself with visits. E.C.I. was a three-hour drive from Baltimore to there.

I was summoned to the Captain's office. Four or five officers surrounded me in a feeble effort to intimidate me. "Jones, what's your fuckin' problem?" the Captain asked.

"I ain't lockin' myself in no muthafuckin' prison cell," I was not trying to be belligerent. "That's the most disrespectful and humiliating thing any man could do. It's like nailing my own coffin shut."

It was decided to place me on cell-restriction until I complied. But that decision was rescinded in less than a week. I had persuaded nearly half the tier to stand with me and protest the injustice of forcing an inmate to lock himself into his own cell. Corrections officers are paid to open and close doors; let them earn their pay.

A number of my fellow prisoners sided with me and two days after, about thirty prisoners refused to lock themselves into their assigned cells. I was placed on Administrative Segregation to await transfer to another prison. While on segregation, I started reading spiritual texts, meditating, exercising, praying and reconciling my thoughts by examining them. I thirsted for freedom. Anyone who tried to stop me would fail.

Chapter XIV

Not Dead, but Ready

I was still alive. I had suffered through a collection of injustices, but until I am summoned to my grave, I cannot command the pity and the support it brings. John Lennon put it best when he sang, "Nobody loves you when you're down and out, but everyone loves you when you're six feet under."

The officials in Hagerstown had tired of me. It was clear that I was never going to be the malleable prisoner they needed me to be. I unsettled inmate populations because I was determined to never adjust to prison. I understood that if I ever got used to prison, I would forever be denied the comforts of freedom and prosperity. I used my gravitas to influence others to think likewise. I could not permit myself to be broken by any of the mechanisms thrust against me. I simply had to endure the myriad of painful emotions that failed relationships left. I had to stand strong against being treated as if I was insignificant and unworthy of anyone's time, attention and affection. I understood why **a man without a family outside trembles in the cold.**

The gauntlet had been thrown down. The parole board had condemned me to another fifteen years of hopelessness. At the time of my parole hearing, I had been in prison for nearly twenty years. I did not expect to be immediately paroled, but when the board ruled that I would not be scheduled to be reconsidered for parole until 2018, I felt like breaking down.

My trial attorney, Barry Diamond had petitioned the parole board to represent me. He and I felt that it was woefully unjust that the parole board would consider that I served as a hit-man for Larry Lee, a notorious drug-dealer. In court, the state could not establish that I even knew him, let alone carried out murders at his behest. The state's evidence was so weak that Larry Lee was never charged in any role for the murder for which I stood convicted.

There is no appeal for the parole board's decision. I was condemned to rot away in prison for the next fifteen years. I had already finished school. I had my G.E.D. and Bachelor's. I was not eligible to take any vocational training classes. Inmates in the Maryland Division of Corrections had to be within three years or less to their release date to qualify for vocational training. My survival was dependent on building a strong character. I had to prepare myself to endure whatever hardship or misery life had in store for me. A lifetime of imprisonment will spare no one from its harshness.

A most important lesson I gleaned from prison is that in a competitive environment, how the game is played is only important if you are losing. Winners do not contend with rules. They make them up as they go to ensure their own victory. For defeat is dishonorable and death is preferable to dishonor.

It was cold outside, but the sky was clear. It was the perfect day for a drive, and I would have welcomed the long drive from Hagerstown, in western Maryland, to Westover, on the Eastern Shore if the three-hour drive did not represent a return to E.C.I. I thought it was understood that E.C.I. was not for me.

I was among six prisoners being transferred. We were shackled as we sat in the back of a prison transportation van. The others talked about the cars they saw on the road, what they had experienced in Hagerstown and how things would be better, in some respect, at E.C.I. I was the only prisoner on the van who had been to E.C.I.

"You niggas got it twisted," I was chipping away at their delusions. "Hagerstown is ten times better than E.C.I. They got more women at E.C.I. You'll see prettier bitches and all that, but it's fucked up down there."

One of the others on the van, a guy named Baldy, seemed to agree with me. He chimed in, "Yo, I ain't never been in E.C.I., but my brotha be writin' me. He down dere and he said that spot is real fucked-up."

The one thing that we all agreed on was that we would each be able to form our own opinions about E.C.I. soon enough. No one had a right to hold any power over me without my permission. And I would never consent to being controlled as if I was a slave. Once we crossed the Bay Bridge, my mood changed. I did not want to talk. A stillness filled me. I was calm and prepared to meet whatever was set before me with the greatness that was within me.

It was dark and very cold outside when we finally arrived at E.C.I. The property room was closed, so we would have to wait until the next day to be processed into the institution. A captain had walked into the property area and asked one of the transportation officers why was I allowed to travel in a sweat suit.

I was decked out in an all gray Jordan sweat suit and gray Nike sneakers. I stood out from the other five prisoners who had traveled with me. They had been wearing the customary blue jeans and gray prison sweat-shirt or blue dress-style shirt with D.O.C. ostensibly printed across the back.

"Mr. Jones was a last minute add on," the transportation officer explained. "He had on all gray, and we were pressed for time."

The officers exchanged some seemingly tense words. There was a disagreement about the time in which we arrived at E.C.I. and the manner in which I was dressed. The two officers who had transported us were visibly upset and I felt the tension.

"Good luck to you fellows," one of the Hagerstown officers had said as he left.

When the officer from Hagerstown had unlocked the shackles from around my ankles, he stood up, put a hand on my shoulder, and said to me, "Take care of yourself, Arlando." The intimacy of the comment was lost on me. It did not mean anything until days later.

We were given overnight bags, a small fresh mint toothpaste, a toothbrush, soap, towel and washcloth. An E.C.I. officer escorted us to Housing Unit 5. Once we were there, we were assigned to cells on the unit.

We were informed that we would be summoned to property early the next morning and from there, we would likely be placed in other housing units.

The officials at E.C.I. were efficient. At precisely 8:30 the very next morning, I was given a pass and told to report to the property area for orientation and to collect my allowable property.

Once we all arrived at the property area, everyone except me was told to wait in a bullpen until called. My property was going to be the first to be inventoried. I walked into the room. My three boxes were already opened and sitting atop the desk.

"Empty all your property on the desk, Mr. Jones," the tall, white, middle-aged sergeant ordered.

I sensed that the sergeant was a hard-ass, the kind of corrections officer who disliked people in general, but particularly prisoners. I was not prepared to call him a racist. The label is too often misapplied. In any event, I felt an instant abiding dislike for this sergeant. The mustache above his lip looked like Hilter's - he even smelled peculiar.

There were scores of corrections officers I disliked. But a direct order from a corrections officer was to be followed if it was lawful. Therefore, I started emptying my boxes.

"You can't have that radio in this institution," the sergeant snapped.

I held up my radio and told the sergeant, "I purchased this radio through a Division of Corrections approved vender when I was at Roxbury ten years ago, and if you look at the sealed sticker, you'll see that I possessed it here, at this very institution, eighteen months ago."

"I don't care 'bout any of that," the sergeant was livid. "The damn thang is too big and you can't have it. It's gotta be sent home."

There were two other corrections officers in the room and two inmate property workers. They stopped doing whatever they were doing and focused their attention on the sergeant and me. I maintained my poise.

"My radio falls within the measurement of allowable radios," I baited the sergeant.

"I'm confiscatin' your radio," he yelled. "You file all the fuckin' grievances you want. You ain't gettin' that radio."

It had been quite some time since I last used my psychological techniques to advance my own interests. "Sarge, I can see you're upset. Can we start over? What's your name?"

"Can't you read?" the sergeant pointed to the gold-plated name tag on his shirt pocket.

"Sergeant Marshall," I addressed him by his title. "Can you call someone that's more familiar with the rules than you? 'Cause you're a stupid muthafucka!"

Marshall's face turned red with irrepressible rage. He instructed one of the officers to go get the captain. No more than a minute or two had passed before a captain entered the property area. He was white, middle-aged and looked pretty fit.

"You wanna fuckin' supervisor?" Sgt. Marshall arrogantly stated, "There go Captain Carroll."

I understood in that very instant that Captain Carroll would side with Sergeant Marshall no matter what. I could have easily employed logic and reason to make my case, but the truth was beyond all reason.

I took a deep breath to calm myself and say to Capt. Carroll, "I've had this radio for more than ten years. I've even had this radio in this very institution and now I'm being told that it's too big, when in fact, I know it isn't."

"The radio is too big," the expected decision. "Take it and put it in confiscation."

"You just as stupid as this dumb muthafucka," I told him. "Get the warden down here."

In that very instant, one of the officers punched me in the back of my head. Rather than waste motion, I hit Captain Carroll in the face. I felt the bone in his face crack, and he fell to the floor out cold. I then turned in time to catch Sgt. Marshall taking another swing at me. I hit him twice in the face before he fell at my feet.

I had been exercising and regulating my diet while on segregation at Roxbury. I was definitely in the best shape of my life and my fighting skills had not diminished over the years. Those soft-ass white boys had chosen the wrong prisoner to pick on.

I was in a mess of trouble after this encounter. The other two corrections officers had fled from the area and the captain was on the floor, gathering his consciousness. When he attempted to get up from the floor, I stomped the back of his head. I was so furious that it did not matter how much damage I inflicted.

Scores of corrections officers entered the property room. I knew that I would be beaten. There was no need to surrender. I swung my fists at every officer who attempted to subdue me. I was blinded by all of the pepper spray. I felt a barrage of punches collide with my head and face. I soon fell to the concrete floor. More pepper spray was sprayed into my face. I was kicked and punched until I slipped into unconsciousness.

I was dragged along the hard floor, stripped naked and thrown into a cold, desolate cell in the prison's medical isolation unit. Several hours passed. I agonized in the cold as I lay there naked.

Suddenly, an attractive black woman appeared in the light. "Mr. Jones? I'm Dr. Samuels; I'm a psychologist. You'll remain here under observation until it's determined that you're no longer a danger to yourself or any others."

"Dr. Samuels, I've never had a psychological breakdown in my life. I epitomize good mental health. I'm in this hellhole, beaten and cold, as punishment for what those crackers did to me. I wouldn't remain quiescent to their barbaric attack against me. Once I'm released from here, your licensin' agency will be notified that you participated in this shit."

I had enough clearness of mind to not antagonize the psychologist and to threaten her livelihood. It was humbling to stand before that woman in such a disgraceful state. My face was swollen from the beating. My eyes were black and the air-conditioned room forced me into a trembling fit. I had to be pretty pathetic to look at.

Dr. Samuels stared into my eyes. She was trying to assess me, I suppose. I did not say another word. If she declared me a danger, I would have been trapped in that unbearably cold cell for days, as opposed to hours. It was Friday, October 31st. It was possible that I would be stuck in isolation until Monday. I opened my mind to accept that for the next forty-eight hours, I would agonize. I would be cold, hungry and alone. I would be isolated and tortured to the point that I would not even experience God's love. I would be all that I had.

A few hours lapsed before a light-skinned, fairly attractive, female lieutenant came to the cell. She identified herself as the institution's chief investigator. "You caused a lot of damage, Mr. Jones," she announced. "Please come to the door so we can talk."

Ordinarily, I would have been pleased to stand naked before an attractive woman, but I was too badly bruised and beaten to feel confident in my physical appearance. In fact, I felt ugly and weak.

"Miss, ain't nothing I can gain by talkin' to you. Those white boys jumped on me, and I got wid 'em. You already know what happened."

"I want your version of what happened, Mr. Jones," the lieutenant countered.

I got up from the floor with as much confidence as I could feign and walked to the cell door. "That racist-ass sergeant told me that I couldn't have my radio. I told him he was stupid and didn't know what he was talkin' 'bout," I made sure my tone was measured. I didn't want to give her the impression that I was irate and on the verge of a psychotic break. "The captain came. He agreed with the sergeant without even listening, so I told him he's just as ignorant as the sergeant. Then somebody hit me in the back of the head."

"So you're sayin' that you were struck first?" The lieutenant was incredulous. I could not restrain myself, "The only reason I'm here is because I didn't remain quiescent to their attack."

The lieutenant stared at me for what seemed like an eternity. I desired to say more because I knew she wanted to reveal things to me she was not supposed to. There is an impenetrable dichotomy between a prisoner and a corrections officer. Our lives are diametrically opposed to one another's. The lieutenant's livelihood was predicated on stopping me from having any human comfort imaginable. If she caught me drinking an alcoholic beverage to assuage the pain that her colleagues had inflicted, her job dictated that she punish me; that she maintain me on some desolate prison unit. The lieutenant's duty was to make certain that I did not engage in something as fundamentally pleasurable as sex. There was no doubt in my mind that this lieutenant's loyalty was to the officials at E.C.I. She knew that I was a victim of bigotry. She had likely faced it herself, but lacked the courage to challenge it. Very few people are willing to sacrifice their livelihood to do what's morally proper.

I went back to the corner of the cell and curled myself up into a ball. I was in too much physical pain to move around. At some point, I fell asleep because I awoke to a white man dressed in a dark blue suit with a shiny silver badge shaking me. I had not heard the cell door open. "I'm Sergeant Justice from the Internal Affairs Unit. You're being charged with two counts of assault," he said as I looked into the face of an official who was serious about his job.

"I prefer not to talk until I have an attorney," I was too exhausted to engage anyone in more dialogue.

"Good decision," Sgt. Justice stood up and left the cell.

Less than an hour after Justice's departure, a squad of about six to eight officers came into the cell. One of them had a video camera to record the entire affair. "Mr. Jones, here are your underwear and a jumpsuit," I heard an authoritative voice. "You are to get dressed. We will escort you to the segregation unit."

I could not see any of the officers' faces. I was blinded by the bright light emanating from the camera. Not to mention, my eyes were swollen from the beating. "You are to turn around and walk backward to us. If you make any sudden move or turn to face us, you'll be pepper sprayed." I respected the overwhelming display of force. I obeyed every given instruction.

The hate I felt for the officials at E.C.I. was palpable. If I had spoken, my words would have reflected vile emotions. That would not have been in my best interest. I simply endured the pain and humiliation in silence.

When we reached the segregation unit, I felt a degree of relief. There were bed sheets, a blanket, and a mattress for me. A basketball was jammed into the window from the outside to prevent me from closing the window. The prison officials did not want me to have any warmth or protection from the winter. I would have to suffer through the cold, but at least I would not be naked and forced to lie on a concrete floor.

Word had already reached the prisoners on segregation that I had knocked out Sergeant Marshall and Captain Carroll and that I had been badly beaten in return. A number of my fellow prisoners were calling to ask if I was alright. I could hardly breathe or speak. My ribs were severely bruised. The prisoner in the cell next to me proved to be invaluable.

Once I had gathered my senses, I came to the cell door to talk to my neighbor. "Homey, I'm fucked up right now. I can barely stand and I'm hungry. I ain't got shit over here. Whatever help you can give me, I'll appreciate it," I said.

"I'm Maxwell, Tray," I heard the compassion in the voice that had answered me. "I got you."

Maxwell explained my predicament to a few others and within minutes I heard something hit my cell door. Maxwell called to me, "Tray, grab that line outside your door."

I reached for the white string laying on the floor in front of my cell. I pulled it in and enjoyed the three boiled eggs and two slices of bread that were inside the brown paper bag tied to the end of the string. It was difficult for me to eat the sandwich I had made, but I was so famished, I forced it down.

It did not take long for me to fall asleep. I was physically and emotionally drained. The next morning, I awoke to the sound of lunch being served. I stood at the door with the cell light on to indicate that I wanted to eat, but the officers passed over me.

"You whores ain't gonna feed me, huh?" I cried out. "You muthafuckas gonna play food games?"

It was Saturday, November 1, 2003 and raining outside. I wanted to close the window. The heat coming through the vent could not compete with the cold wind blowing through the open window. I was an unapologetic hedonist compelled to exist as an ascetic. It was an unwholesome cruelty. Monday could not have come soon enough. My cell door window was blocked with cardboard. The officers could not look into the cell. I was not being fed or allowed recreation privileges. There was no incentive for me to leave the window unobscured. I was hungry, cold and miserable. Why put that on display? My fellow prisoners had put together a care package for me: a washcloth, toothpaste, toothbrush, soap, a couple novels to read and a few boiled eggs to eat.

"Remove the cardboard from your window," I heard the official command.

"Why?" I asked. "You gonna feed me? Let me shower?"

"Until you remove that cardboard from the window, there is absolutely nothing we can talk about," he said.

I got up from the bunk and removed the cardboard from the window. A white man wearing a black T-shirt, black uniform pants and boots stood outside. He was a well-groomed man with piercing brown eyes.

"My window is blocked 'cause I'm miserable. The police ain't feedin' me and I can't get any rec time."

"Who said you can't rec? And why haven't you been eatin'?" The official asked.

"I came over here Friday night," I started explaining. "I got into a fight with your fellow officers 'round property."

"I'm Captain West," the official introduced himself. "I know exactly why you're here. Now you say my officers haven't fed you?"

I told Captain West that I was denied breakfast, lunch and dinner. I would have my light on, nothing obscuring the window, standing at the door to receive my meal, but the officers consistently passed over me. They refused to feed me. My fellow prisoners have shared their food with me. Captain West assured me that that mistreatment would immediately stop. He ordered the dietary department to send me a tray. He had a conversation with the officers who worked on the segregation unit and instructed them to feed me and afford me the same recreation and shower privileges as everyone else. Moreover, he had the property officer give me all of my allowable property: books, cosmetics and underclothing. The most important thing was that he removed the basketball from the window so that I could shut it to allow the cell to warm up.

Captain West communicated to me that Captain Carroll and Sergeant Marshall were bigots. He understood that they were assholes and said he was sorry that I had to face these unfortunate circumstances. I was not the first person to be treated badly by those two, but I was the first to attack them.

Experience had already revealed to me that no one gets exonerated after assaulting an officer. I had assaulted five or six of them. The lieutenant who spoke to me while I was in medical isolation had told me that Sgt. Marshall's jaw was broken and

Capt. Carroll had had a seizure when I stomped his head into the concrete floor. I was definitely in a lot of trouble. Years would pass before I would be allowed back into a general population.

The regrets started entering my mind. I should have surrendered the radio. I would have won a grievance and had it returned to me. Damn! I ain't have a wife, my ribs were bruised, and I labored to breathe. Captain West assured me that I would not be treated harshly because I assaulted the officers in the property room. What happened there was inevitable.

After about two weeks, I received a note from Francine informing me that she was filing for divorce. She condemned me for being immature and stuck in my "street ways." My marriage was over long before I received the note, but it was the worst possible news at that time. The adjustment hearing officer had sanctioned me to 720 days in segregation and an indefinite loss of visiting privileges. I was also formally charged with two counts of assault, one in the first degree and the other in the second degree. I faced an additional one hundred years.

My indomitable spirit was under attack. It was during this time that Momma Boo provided me with some much-needed assurance of love. Without her, I would not have survived. When I complained about my hardships, Momma Boo said, "Cry me river, build a bridge and get over it." Everything I would need in life I was born with. God made no mistakes in His Creation. There was within me a creative ability and strength beyond even my own comprehension. I had to know that I was great and worthy of far more than what I had been given. The only one able to communicate that to me was Momma Boo.

In segregation, faced with divorce, the threat of having an additional one hundred years added to my life sentence, in excruciating pain with a pair of swollen eyes and cut-up lips, I thought that death was the best way to end my suffering. Better men than myself, World and Avery, to name only two, had chosen death over an endless lifetime of suffering.

I understood that my death would cause Momma Boo tremendous grief. Others might mourn me for a day or two, but Momma Boo would have hurt at her core if I killed myself. She believed in me and told me to believe in myself. What can I say? It was Momma Boo and my birth mother who convinced me that my pink lips are pretty; they aren't ugly and shameful, as I had once believed.

Since I knew that my death would cause Momma Boo grief, I did not kill myself.

"When you love someone, you should never deliberately hurt her, Tray," Momma Boo had said that to me when I was plotting revenge on Francine for the slight she had heaved on me. "It's gonna be enough pain and hurt in y'all's relationship on its own."

Love brings its own hurt. Thus, to deliberately inflict pain on someone you claim to love should never be forgiven. George Bernard Shaw even observed, "If you strike a child, take care that you strike it in anger, even at the risk of maiming it for life. A blow in cold blood neither can nor should be forgiven."

I had vowed to never deliberately hurt Momma Boo. It was a matter of reciprocity. Even though death was titillating with its promise to end my suffering and misery; I could not deliberately hurt my Momma Boo — I had to fight on. I needed a tool with which to fight. I chose love as my tool. Leo Tolstoy had influenced me when he wrote: **more difficult and more blessed than all else is to love this life in one's sufferings, in**

undeserved sufferings. What could I do with love aside from cry a river, build a bridge, and get over it.

Chapter XV

Love Life and Live it

Niggas with an Attitude, (N.W.A.), a popular rap group from the late 1980s coined lyrics that seemed to capture the essence of life as I knew it to be when they said, "It's plain to see, you can't change me, I'm gonna be a nigga fo' life." The classification team at Eastern Correctional Institution determined for the second time that I was unfit for their facility. I was incorrigible. And so, I was transferred to Jessup's maximum-security prison.

I knew most of the prisoners at J.C.I. I had been with many of them at the penitentiary or at the Maryland House of Corrections. It was very unusual for a prisoner to be transferred into a penal institution from another if the prisoner had punitive segregation time to serve. It was customary for a prisoner to serve out his segregation time at the facility where he received it before a transfer was permitted. But nothing had been customary about my journey thus far. I was at an odd point in life. I understood that I was more than just mind and body. I had a well-developed intellect, which meant I was too smart to fully appreciate that I did not know the world well at all. My strategy of maintaining a relationship with a woman had failed.

My charisma and my smile were not enough to keep me from being at odds with prison officials or to win a favorable decision from the parole board.

When I arrived at J.C.I., I was promptly put into a segregation cell. I did not have the energy to be angry. The prison grapevine had told the story about what happened at E.C.I. My place among the "bad-ass-niggas" in the joint was solid in the pantheons. I did not have enough focus to appreciate the loving camaraderie offered to me by those I had not seen in years. I resolved that I would never again get on my knees to pray and whine to that uncaring and icily indifferent god that folks kept telling me to trust and believe in. He was not listening. I would only communicate with the God that created me.

I simply sat still. My body was starting to heal. The physical pain from the beating I had received began to subside. I was numb. Life had hit me with treacherous and sadistic blows. I was armed with ample enough translative information to keep me from a psychotic break. I trusted that what was inside of me was better than all that was behind me and before me. While my religious beliefs had been called into question because I had ignored ritualistic forms of worship, my spiritual conviction was not. The True God would not place a burden on me greater than I could bear. Words that I had read in Leo Tolstoy's *War and Peace* were resounding through my mind.

A character, Pierre, had mused, "Life is everything. Life is God. Everything changes and moves to and fro, and that movement is God. And while there is life, there is joy in consciousness of the Godhead. To love life is to love God. More difficult and more blessed than all else is to love this life in one's sufferings, in undeserved sufferings."

I felt that life had dealt me a terrible hand, but I had played it as best I knew how. While some of the misery and suffering that I had endured and had to endure were self-inflicted, most were inflicted by forces outside of my control. Of course, that is okay. Bad things happened to good people just as good things happened to bad people. If life was not the way I wanted it to be, then I had to situate things as I desired them to be. We come into this world endowed with the necessary tools to find fulfillment and happiness for ourselves. But too often we squander our divine gifts as Jesus spoke of when he offered the parable of The Prodigal Son.

There was no point in counting the days that I had to spend in segregation. The tedium of each day would grow stronger. I could easily count down a 90-day, or even twice that, a 180-day stint in segregation. But 720 days was too much. I simply had to be still and let each moment of each day present to me what it would. Initially, I fought the tedium. I hurled vulgarities at it. I read cheap novels, participated in petty arguments with other inmates, sparked chaotic conversations, fantasized about a better future and did physical exercises in a feeble effort to best the tedium.

Serendipity finally struck. I woke up during the wee hours. I cannot recall if there were any conversations happening on the tier. Folks were always chatting about one thing or another through the air vents or outside the cell doors. It was hardly ever absolutely quiet on segregation tiers. But a quiet invaded my consciousness; it was absolutely tantalizing to the point of titillation. I sat up on my bunk cross-legged with my back flat against the wall and listed to the silence.

The quiet communicated to me a transformative message. The message had no words that I can articulate, but it told me simply that every experience I had, I had to have. It was okay that I had regrets, but it was not okay to harbor resentment or bitterness. Each moment that I breathed was God's gift to me. It is imperative that I do not squander my gift by doing that which God does not desire from me.

If I wanted to best the loneliness, I had to love. I did not necessarily have to have an object to love. But I had to love. No greater tool than love was forged to accomplish man's greatest desire: To be loved. To be accepted completely with all your flaws, imperfections and human inadequacies.

It came to me that genuine love was not the maudlin or romantic thing that I had associated with it. Love was simply that: Love. It had no equivalent word. Every descriptive word I could use to help develop another's understanding of love would serve only to take away from love's true meaning. Jesus Christ best exemplified love by embodying it.

When people around you or even intimately involved with your life do not appreciate you or recognize your worth, you notice theirs. Love demands that you make those near you better. Even if no one will love you more than you love them. That is okay. Genuine love provides inexhaustible power and energy. Whatever suffering that must be done will be bearable if you suffer in love.

Stay in the exact moment that you are in RIGHT NOW, at the present moment, and you will experience God's gift to you, the Present. Whenever you are angry about something, it is a matter that has already occurred - five seconds ago, five minutes ago, five years ago or even fifty years ago. Anger and its concomitant emotions (resentment, hatred, etc.) will eviscerate anyone who harbors them. As powerful as God is, He does not change the past. So why begrudge what is done? Summon the love within you and lovingly look at what was done, then return to right now in order to receive your gift. You will notice at any instant that the "gifted" moment contains nothing that angers you or threatens your serenity.

If fear or anxiety overwhelms you, it is because of something that has not occurred. Only anticipated or supposed events can cause frustration, fear or anxiety: When I get to work, I know my boss is gonna fire me ... when I get home, I know my children will be acting a fool.... I can give examples into infinity. Suffice to say, if you have read this far into my book, you have my point.

This moment is where love resides; its potency is at its fullest when you seek first to understand a situation or a person before judging. For instance, it would have changed things had I understood that Sergeant Marshall likely grew up dirt poor on Maryland's eastern shore. He possessed no sophistication. Sgt. Marshall was probably reared to believe that hating others somehow elevated his social standing. And that hatred, which is at the core of his world view, pushes away from him the one thing that he desires most, to be loved.

A profound understanding of a person's greatest worth when it is executed in the present moment. The wisest among us is recognized for his compassion and understanding; for the essence of wisdom is compassion. Moreover, it is not possible to genuinely understand another and withhold compassion from him or her.

No one has to do anything exotic or go to any extremes to attain wisdom. Simply live in the now, the Moment, the Present and appreciate God's eternal gift. Eckhart Tolle brilliantly discussed the value of this in *The Power of Now*.

Some people will use demagoguery to mislead us. Our ego typically convinces us that we are so remarkably intelligent and insightful that very few can appreciate the sophisticated tenets of this religiosity of that philosophy. We needlessly complicate life because of vanity. If you live in the moment and fully accept the gift that the present forever gives you, all the power and understanding of the universe will avail itself to you.

Of course, it is difficult to focus your full attention on the one thing you are doing or the one person you are with. Our vanity demands that we devote our brilliant minds to more than a single thing at a time. If I am talking to someone, I can surely think about what I will do once this conversation ends. Worse, I could transfer my focus to something or someone who angered me five seconds ago - fifty years ago even.

The past tends to be quite seductive. The past's vortex is so strong, anyone among us can be pulled in by its force. A willingness to stay focused on the now we have been allotted can keep us wise and thereby equipped with what is needed to love life and enjoy all that it presents.

When I entered that hospice care room to serve Hakim, I sat in the moment and took advantage of all the power that the eternal now presents. None of the philosophies or theologies that I was familiar with at the time seemed adequate enough to express how I felt. I stopped and stayed exactly where I was and looked into Hakim's eyes and the now came as I needed compassion, courage and understanding. **Do what you are supposed to do at the very moment you are to do it.** This seems far too simple for our complex minds. The more complicated we make things, the more adoration we should receive when we demonstrate a mastery of the complication we have created. How genius is that?

Tolstoy tells a simple parable, "The Three Questions," about a king who seeks an answer to the most important thing to do. Who is the most important person to listen to? And what is the best time to do a thing? Do whatever you are doing with focus. If you are conversing with someone, listen and be with that person. No one else is more important than who is with you at that moment. And, of course, RIGHT NOW is always the best time to do anything.

The demagogues have persuaded the masses that truth presents itself with bombast and one grandiloquent statement after another. That which is simple, pure and bowed by humility is wrong. The truth is complicated and belongs only to those capable of sophistication. Those who present themselves as pure and humble are treated as provincial.

Why develop complex rituals and tomes of philosophies and enshrine monuments and cathedrals? "Keep It Simple Stupid (KISS)", any Narcotic's Anonymous group can give that very sacred teaching. I received a profound lesson from Guru Maya through a correspondence course.

If we live in ignorance, our life is simply a series of human experiences. If we live with the awareness of the Shakti (Divine Truth), our life is a jigsaw puzzle leading to freedom once we understand each piece in relationship to the whole.

In our fiendish effort to be separate and distinguished from everyone else, we find ourselves leading a commonly ignorant life. We find it nearly impossible to meet the first and last demand of genius, which is to love truth. We do ourselves a disservice by ignoring Nietzsche's wise observation, "A man of genius is unbearable unless he possesses at least two things: gratitude and purity."

When I entered Hakim's room, I entered into the moment. The sophisticated philosophies and theological tenets that I had acquainted myself with through diligent study proved to be insignificant. The simplicity and wisdom encompassed by the now endowed me with all that I needed to comfort my friend. That very simplicity and wisdom that served me well with Hakim got me through segregation and every other difficult circumstance I got myself into.

All the power that we will ever need in order to lead fulfilling lives is available to us at every given moment. Divine truth does not come to us by mysterious revelation, in some kind of earth-shattering manner. It comes to us in a simple, yet revealing way. Enlightenment is all around us - everything within your sight can be looked into for the purpose of affording you insight. But of course, too much insight can inspire you to boast enlightenment, which leads to the brilliant lights and entertainment. In other words, be wary of those who articulate their experiences with eloquence simply to dazzle audiences and earn an income. True wisdom is communicated through love — and rewards itself.

I do not begrudge entertainers. They add aesthetic to life. Entertainment does wonders for the soul. The human mind must be entertained. Without entertainment, we would become dull and would not produce enough inspiration in this world to make manifest the warmth and beauty that comforts the many.

The world is simply how it was created. If you are an optimist, you will truthfully declare that we are living in the best of all possible worlds. An equally honest pessimist will bemoan the truthfulness of that. And so, the world is as we perceive it - perfect or imperfect. It is perhaps both. All things beget their meaning from their opposites. The *Tao Te Ching* captures it best:

> When people see some things as beautiful, other things become ugly.
> When people see some things as good, other things become bad.
> Being and non-being create each other.
> Difficult and easy support each other.
> Long and short define each other.
> Before and after follow each other...

As we journey this life, we take on information that is either translative or transformative. The translative, soothing information will allow you, for the most part, to feel comfortable about your beliefs, your actions, and your ossified rituals. Transformative information shatters all that you hold too dear. Transformation demands that you transcend this mundane world even if you are compelled to live in it. Transformation dictates that you love, that you present yourself in such a humble manner that you offer folks the power to destroy you and the trust that they will not.

Transformation means allowing each moment to die so that you may reap the benefits from the forever present.

Transformative information is available to everyone. It only seems that those of us who suffer through life's greatest crucibles experience its fruits.

Life is constantly moving; all motion is life. Learn to love life - all that moves and changes - and you will know a joy that transcends the emotions that consistently change. You will experience bliss, a magnificent state of being that is void of fickle emotions. When you love life, sadness and all the other emotions will be no different from happiness. Bliss is an integral part of God's gift, which is always available. It cannot be attained at any time other than right now. The past is an obsessive source of anger. The future inspires anxiety. The present holds serenity, clarity, and all the wisdom you will need to propel you forward on this sacred journey—life.

About the Author

Arlando "Tray" Jones, III is serving a life sentence at the Jessup Correctional Institution in Maryland. While in prison, Tray has educated himself through a program offered by Coppin State University, graduating *cum laude* with a B.A. degree in Applied Psychology. He went on to take an extensive college-level curriculum in the Humanities through the JCI Scholars Program. He is the author of *Eager Street: A Life on the Corner and Behind Bars* (2010), and he was featured in Dr. Drew Leder's book, *The Soul Knows No Bars* (2000). He hopes his story convinces people, including young urban men, that life on the corner dealing in crime and violence is not glamorous, but a ticket to a life behind bars.

"Every person will experience at least one great challenge. That challenge will have its ups and downs, highs and lows. No one can avoid life's inevitable great challenge. Therefore, no one is likely to be measured or judged by the challenge he faces. Each person is only measured or judged by the way he or she responds to that great challenge."

Apprentice House is the country's only campus-based, student-staffed book publishing company. Directed by professors and industry professionals, it is a nonprofit activity of the Communication Department at Loyola University Maryland.

Using state-of-the-art technology and an experiential learning model of education, Apprentice House publishes books in untraditional ways. This dual responsibility as publishers and educators creates an unprecedented collaborative environment among faculty and students, while teaching tomorrow's editors, designers, and marketers.

Outside of class, progress on book projects is carried forth by the AH Book Publishing Club, a co-curricular campus organization supported by Loyola University Maryland's Office of Student Activities.

Eclectic and provocative, Apprentice House titles intend to entertain as well as spark dialogue on a variety of topics. Financial contributions to sustain the press's work are welcomed. Contributions are tax deductible to the fullest extent allowed by the IRS.

To learn more about Apprentice House books or to obtain submission guidelines, please visit www.apprenticehouse.com.

Apprentice House
Communication Department
Loyola University Maryland
4501 N. Charles Street
Baltimore, MD 21210
Ph: 410-617-5265 • Fax: 410-617-2198
info@apprenticehouse.com•www.apprenticehouse.com

www.ingramcontent.com/pod-product-compliance
Lightning Source LLC
LaVergne TN
LVHW091635100826
845152LV00002B/37

* 9 7 8 1 6 2 7 2 0 2 3 8 1 *